Frank J. Ki

The Secret of
Quantum
Living

From the author of
The Secret of Instant Healing

This book is not intended to diagnose, prescribe or treat. The information contained herein is in no way to be considered as a substitute for care from a duly licensed healthcare professional.

LucidSea

THE SECRET OF QUANTUM LIVING
ISBN: 978-0-9844264-1-6
ISBN: 0-9844264-1-8

Cover design by Andrea Barth of Guter-Punkt
www.guter-punkt.de
Illustrations by Martina Kinslow
Interior design by Lynn Stuart
Editing by Christy Heitger-Ewing

Printed in the U.S.A.

Printed March 7, 2010

Contents

Preface

Two years ago, I developed Quantum Entrainment (QE), a unique process for Self exploration that bypasses many of the pitfalls of inner work by reducing all created things, physical and mental, down to their most basic constituent, pure awareness. Initially, I focused on the remarkable healing effects that we humans are capable of performing, but rarely demonstrate, with just a subtle shift in awareness. I wrote *The Secret of Instant Healing* so that anyone who wished could learn to heal with QE. Since its writing, people all over the world have learned and experienced the joys of healing with QE. I have been overwhelmed by the remarkable stories of healing events exuberant readers have shared with me.

I did not want *The Secret of Quantum Living* to be a rehashing or an extension of what you have already learned. I wanted this book to uncover something new and vital to enrich your life in broader and deeper ways. Initially, I was not sure if I could communicate to you, the reader, the subtleties of pure QE through the written word. It turns out that my concern was unfounded. The initial reaction I have received from those previewing this book and practicing the refined process of QE laid down herein has far exceeded my expectations. Both experienced QE-ers and readers completely new to the QE Process found the reading of *The Secret of Quantum Living* to encourage a profound shift in the way they approach their lives. They felt a new, more solid foundation had been created in their awareness which resulted in less conflict and more confidence, less disharmony and greater peace, less need to seize control and a greater appreciation for life just as it is. In short, they watched as the impediments in their lives gave way to reveal

1

their basic inner goodness, the shining of their Self.

In *The Secret of Quantum Living*, you will discover how to apply the QE process to help improve vital areas in your life, such as financial worries, anger issues, and overall negativity. QE can also improve your relationships, your sex life, and your eating, sleeping, and exercising habits. While healing will also be addressed in this book, if you are interested in learning the art and science of the QE rapid healing process, then *The Secret of Instant Healing* is still your best resource.

The Secret of Quantum Living is divided into two sections followed by appendices and a glossary. Appendix A contains frequently asked questions sent to me from readers around the globe. The questions will have real value once you have begun integrating QE into your daily activity. Appendix B is autobiographical and tells the story of how QE came to be developed. I would not normally write about myself unless the story enriched the experience of the reader in some way. I have been asked how I came to develop QE so many times, however, that I thought I would answer the question in Appendix B. I feel the Glossary has significant value. Much of the terminology I use is in common use but rarely defined by the author as to its specific application. Much confusion can be avoided by taking a few minutes to peruse the glossary for definitive definitions of words and phrases as applied to my teaching. While I try to define new words and phrases in the text, I strongly encourage you to frequently refer to the glossary until you own the definition for yourself.

In Section I, *Quantum Entrainment*, you will be introduced to a series of simple and effective progressive exercises culminating in the pure QE process. For this reason, I suggest that you read Section I from beginning to end without skipping ahead. For those of you who have read *The Secret of Instant Healing*, some of the material will be familiar. This has value on two levels. First, it is necessary for the new reader to know this material in preparation for easily learning and effectively performing the QE process. Second, it is an excellent review for those of you who are already practicing QE. This review establishes a valuable grounding for the seasoned QE-er to learn pure QE, a refinement in the QE process itself. Pure QE encourages your awareness to expand beyond imposed boundaries for seamless expression of QE into everyday living.

Section I offers new insights and explanations for the inner workings of the QE Process that will expand the mind of, and I think excite, the seasoned QE-er. For those readers exposed to this simple and successful philosophy for the first time, well, I believe you are in for a real treat. In this first section, you will explore the role of Eufeeling and its relationship with pure awareness. You will also learn about the inward and outward paths to happiness and, because the QE process quickly induces higher states of consciousness, we will discuss what to look for as your perception refines toward enlightenment.

In Section II, *Quantum Living*, you will discover how to apply what you have learned in the first part of the book. Now you will test pure QE for its practical value. Section II provides the basics for living in pure awareness and offers the exciting opportunity to find the peace and bliss of your Eufeeling reflecting back to you from the people, objects, and events that comprise your everyday life. Living with QE, one finds the mundane life permeated with a sense of awe and quiet expectation.

I am very excited about the potential impact this book can have on your life and our world. QE opens our awareness to our inner Self in a unique and effective way. By opening our inner self awareness, we are returned to the newness of childhood with eyes full of wonder at the ordinary beauty that permeates our lives. Our world has been living under a kind of darkness of the soul. We have been peering outward into that darkness for resolution when the answer lies in another direction, toward the light of Self. With the opening of this book, one more candle has been lit against that darkness.

Frank Kinslow
Sarasota, Florida
October 8, 2009

SECTION I
Quantum Entrainment

CHAPTER ONE

Miracles

"Expectancy is the atmosphere for miracles."
Edwin Louis Cole

Subject and object are only one. The barrier between them cannot be said to have broken down as a result of recent experience in the physical sciences, for this barrier does not exist.
Erwin Schrodinger

Place the tip of your index finger lightly in the middle of your forehead. Now pay close attention to what you feel there. What does your finger feel like against your forehead? What does your forehead feel like against your finger? Is your forehead warm or cold? Is your skin dry or oily? Is there a pulse in your finger? Is there a pulse on your forehead? Quietly, but very clearly, pay attention to what is taking place where finger and forehead meet. Do this for 30 seconds.

Now, how do you feel? Is your body a little more relaxed? Is your mind a little more peaceful? Certainly your mind is more centered, less scattered. Isn't this true? Before you started reading the above paragraph, your mind was moving more. You may have been anticipating what you were going to learn from this book. Or you may have been thinking about the meal you just ate or are going to eat, you may have been contemplating an earlier conversation with a friend or thinking about what you have to do to get ready for your trip next week. But during this simple exercise, your mind was purely present. Your awareness was simple and direct. And, as a result, your body relaxed and your mind became more peaceful. Why is that? How can a slight shift in awareness make such an immediate and positive change in your body and mind?

Well, I'm glad you asked. Stick with me through the pages of this simple but profound little book and you will learn how to wield the power of awareness to transform your life in every way. That's right. Every aspect of your life, health, finances, love, work, and spiritual pursuits will all be made lively and full; all you have to do is learn how to be aware. And by the way, learning to be aware is just about the simplest thing you can do.

By learning how to be aware in just the right way, you will be able to heal physical complaints like sprained knees, headaches, indigestion, and aching joints; quell emotional concerns like jealousy, grief, anxiety, and fear; and take control of your finances, relationships, and even your sex life. It even works on your pets. The process I will teach you is simple, scientific, easily learned, and immediately effective. It does not require that you sit in meditation, bend your body in uneasy postures, or force your breath to conform in any way. You do not have to join a group or pay dues. It does not even require that you believe in it for it to work. It is beyond belief. It is Quantum Entrainment (QE) and it is opening hearts and minds all over the world to the harmonizing power of pure awareness.

Do I have your attention? Did I get you to put down that turkey sandwich and wipe the mayo from the corner of your mouth? Good. Attention is all you need to make QE work. That's it. That's just how simple it is. I will show you how to move away from the thought-strewn, multi-directional mind into the calm sea of pure awareness so that you may experience first-hand freedom from mental turmoil and emotional madness. As the Bhagavad-Ghita puts it, "Just a little pure awareness relieves a soul of great fear." The wisdom of the ancients is here at your fingertips within the pages of this book.

I've made some pretty strong statements so far, and I wouldn't do this if I couldn't back up my words with some pretty strong action. So, I think I've gabbed enough for now. I would like you to experience the remarkable effect that focused pure awareness can have on your body. Follow these steps closely and you will be amazed at what you can already do...and this is just the beginning.

The Growing Finger Exercise

Hold up your hand, palm facing you, and find the horizontal line, or crease, that runs along the bottom of your hand at the top of your wrist. Find the same horizontal crease on your other hand. Place your wrists together so that the two creases line up exactly with each other. Now, carefully bring your palms and fingers together. Your hands should line up perfectly in prayer-like fashion.

Look at how your two middle fingers line up. They will either be even in length or one will be shorter than the other. For this exercise, you will pick the shorter finger. If your fingers are even, you get to choose either the right or the left one. That's up to you.

Separate your hands and place them on the table or in your lap. Look at, and become aware of, the middle finger that you chose and think one time, "This finger will grow longer." Now, don't move the finger. Just become acutely aware of it. Do this for one full minute. You don't have to tell it to grow longer again. Once is enough. Just provide what it needs to make the transition: *focused awareness*. That one finger gets your total attention for one full minute. That is all!

After one minute has passed, again measure the length of your fingers using the creases across your wrists exactly as you did before. Presto-Chango: your finger is longer! It's amazing. It's like a little miracle. However, St. Augustine taught, "Miracles do not happen in contradiction to nature but only in contradiction to what is *known* in nature." So, get used to it. You will be producing little miracles every day once you "know" the secret of awareness.

Before the Growing Finger Exercise, you told yourself what you wanted to happen, didn't you? You had a single thought, "This finger will grow longer." And then it happened without any further work, mental or physical, on your part. The only ingredient you added was awareness. This is all we ever need to get things done. I know that is hard to believe, but it is true and you will prove it to yourself by the time you finish reading this book. Awareness is the prime mover of all that we know, see, and feel and once you become aware of that, your life will flow effortlessly like a river to merge with the sea of all possibilities.

Now think back to when you first realized that your finger was longer. What did you feel at that very moment? Did you feel surprised? Did you feel a sense of awe and wonder? A miracle has that effect on us, doesn't it? It wakes us from our sleepwalking. For a moment, we are moved, excited, and inspired. Wouldn't it be a marvel if we could live our lives in constant wonderment like an innocent child exploring her world with eyes wide open? Well, guess what? We can. Albert Einstein knew this secret. "There are only two ways to live your life," he said. "One is as if nothing is a miracle. The other is as if everything is a miracle."

Now, let me spend a minute more on this feeling of wonderment because it is a very important piece to the loving and living puzzle. That feeling of wonder or awe is what I call a Eufeeling. A Eufeeling is proof that we have dived into the waters of absolute pure awareness and have reemerged bathed in its regenerative and harmonizing influence. The Eufeeling is a vital part of learning how to master your life without doing a thing. The Eufeeling always feels good so get used to the idea of filling your life with greater and greater peace, love, and joy. A little later we will spend more time understanding and experiencing the Eufeeling. As you follow the simple instructions laid out in the pages of this little book, you will gain the tools and the insight to transform the lives of your family and friends and even strangers. In a matter of seconds, you can touch them deeply and forever. And each time, in doing so, you will have also transformed yourself. It cannot happen any other way.

This is my promise to you. Learn the QE Process and perform it as it is presented herein and you will soon find remarkable changes taking place in all areas of your life. Some changes you will expect, but most will be like a gift you were not expecting. You will continually be surprised by joy and quelled by your own inner peace. Everything in your life will be exactly the same and yet, somehow more friendly and sustaining. Your friends may remark that you are different, more present, more giving. To you, the problems—the highs and lows that dogged and defined your previous life—are now met with an inner acceptance that allows them to flow easily in and out without resistance. Inner peace is the rule rather than a highly sought-after and rarely experienced exception. Your inner life will become remarkably different while outwardly you may not appear to change at all, except maybe for more relaxed shoulders, a comfortable, confident gait, and, most evident of all, an impish sparkle in your eyes. Then, before long, you will look back over your life and think to yourself, "I am the miracle."

CHAPTER TWO

How to Become Happy

Shortage of time is the greatest shortage of our time.
Fred Polak

Thousands of candles can be lighted from a single candle,
and the life of the candle will not be shortened.
Happiness never decreases by being shared.
Buddha

If you ask ten people what "living in the now" means, you will get ten different answers. Like the weather, everybody is talking about it but no one seems to be doing much about it. Maybe that is because many of us aren't even sure what "living in the now" means or what benefit it could possibly provide us.

At first glance, it would seem that defining "the now" would be an easy chore, but it has not turned out that way. You might say, "Now is now," and let it go at that. You would be one of the smart ones. Scratching even a little below the "what is now" surface reveals a writhing tangle of rational but unmanageable worms ready to confound scientist and philosopher alike. In fact, the quest for present awareness and the illusive inner peace it is reported to reveal has baffled humankind since the first spark of self-awareness burned in those most ancient of human eyes.

Our bodies/minds evolved around short-term stresses like unexpected bad weather, minor skirmishes with neighboring tribes, and the

13

occasional hike up a tall tree to avoid being skewered by a Saber Tooth Tiger. Prehistoric hunter-gatherers worked only three or four days a week to provide the necessities for survival. Sandwiched between stressful events laid days of idle socialization with clan members, lazy walks by the lake, and hours of horizontal cloud watching.

If we could choose one word that would define the lives of modern humans, it would have to be hectic. When, in recorded history, have we been so predisposed to incessant activity? We truly are driving ourselves insane. Sixty or seventy years is not enough time for our nerves and bones and brains to adapt to the increased activity and stress that modern living has thrust upon us. Our body/minds have experienced had the generations of gentle evolution needed to prepare for the onslaught of 21st century living. They were made for a more peaceful, contemplative existence.

That contemplative nature born of our earliest forefathers is with us still, genetically coded in our every cell, patiently waiting to be redis-covered. It is an ever-present but frail voice, straining against the ever-escalating rumble of modern madness. If you take a moment to listen, you can hear it quietly pleading, "Slow down! Enjoy. Let the world pass you by just a few minutes more." This voice can be heard, not echoing in our past or reflected in the hopes and fears of our imagined future, but right now. And that brings us back to now.

We feel that if we take time to do nothing, that is time wasted. This problem is not a matter of quantity but quality. Turning inward rejuvenates the mind and body in a way that harmonizes them with the outside world. Taking time to daydream or meditate will more than make up for "lost" time in renewed energy and creativity.

Daily activity is inescapable, and while retiring from the world to meditate will certainly yield benefits, we have missed a greater truth. We have wrongly assumed that we cannot be both active and quiet at the same time. As it turns out, we can be both outwardly active while inwardly at rest. Yes, you can have your cake and eat it, too. By virtue of being human, you can actually rejuvenate as you go; you can maintain a state of restful inner peace *while* engaged in your daily routine.

Picture a man lying on his back looking up at the stars. He's been lying there for a long time and his mind is like the quiet emptiness of space. This is not the mind of a businessman or a factory worker. This man wouldn't know how to open a door, eat soup with a spoon, or utter a civil salutation. And yet he is fully aware and filled with a confidence and calm that has previously been reserved for saints and great spiritual teachers. This man died eons ago wrapped in animal skins and grieved over by a handful of others like him—members of his clan. His contemplative life was in stark contrast to his present-day counterpart whose thoughts reflect a knot of wriggling snakes rather than the motion of the stars. Contemporary man's synaptic brain junctions are fervently firing from the first flicker of awareness in the morning to its last gasp at night when the welcome silence of sleep releases him and prepares him for the onslaught of the coming of day.

Our ancient ancestor was basically like us. For all practical intents and purposes, he was us. If he were born today and raised in a middle class family, I don't think you would be able to pick him out in a class of his contemporary cousins. But here is the problem. The forces that forged his large brain and upright body are not the ones modern man knows today—not even close. Our bodies and minds, formed before time was invented, are today subjected to foreign forces unknown to ancient peoples. Pollution, high-stress jobs, the pressure to multi-task, a soaring divorce rate, hours of sitting in front of a computer, and the need to digest on a daily basis the negative news shared from around the world were all unknown stressors our ancestors did not have to face even a hundred years ago.

To say that we have created a hectic world is to state the obvious. We are driven by an insatiable need to fill all voids. Knowledge is the new god. We feel that if we know about something, then we own it and can control it. And if we can control a thing, we can either use it to further our knowledge and increase control or protect ourselves from harm—both real and imagined. So our collective thinking goes something like this: If we increase our knowledge about something, then we can increase our control over it. If we increase our control over a thing we can use it for further knowledge or eliminate it as a threat to our safety and continued search for knowledge. Do you see the subtle insanity intimately woven into the very fabric of our thinking?

The question we should be asking ourselves is not, "How can I get more control?" The primary question that every one of us should entertain is, "How can I be free of the need to control?" Beyond the basic needs for survival and life's creature comforts, why do we *need* to make more money, drive a faster car, or feel compelled to share our problems with the check-out clerk at the convenience store? Abraham Maslow would say we have a psychological need to control and he would be right. But that begs the question, "What causes the psychological need for control?"

The need to control comes from the feeling that control is needed. That is, we feel out of control. The feeling may or may not be conscious. In fact, most often it is not. But that subtle, unconscious need to be in control fuels most of our desires beyond mere survival and basic comfort. (Now, I realize this model is a gross oversimplification of the intricate psychological interactions bouncing around between our ears, but stick with me awhile and let's see where this is headed. No pun intended.)

Ego is expressed in one of two ways. It can be at rest, feeling expanded and complete. You experience this when you look deeply into a star-filled sky or when you wake up and feel in sync—like everything is just right with the world. The other expression of ego is the one we experience 99% of the time. That is the ego that feels empty and tries to fill that emptiness by gathering around it the things and people that make if temporarily feel full.

That is the key word: "temporarily." We don't seem to be able to appease the ego permanently, do we? When we buy a new car, our ego is completely content only until we get a dent in the door or have to make the first payment. By the time we make the last payment, we can't wait to get rid of that car and buy a new one. New car, new job, new foods, more money, more time, more love; our egos relentlessly seek more and new experiences in an inane effort to drown out that wee, tiny voice from somewhere deep within us that keeps whispering, "I'm not full yet."

You might think that this feeling of emptiness is not a good thing, but it really is. Just like physical pain is a good thing because if we didn't feel pain, we wouldn't know that something was hurt. Imagine if you had a neurological deficit or the genetic disease anhidrosis where you could not feel pain. (Anhidrosis actually means the inability to sweat which accompanies the inability to feel pain.) You couldn't safely drink or eat hot foods, and even if you did, you wouldn't know if you were chewing your tongue along with a fork full of steak. You wouldn't know if you were developing frostbite from a leisurely walk in the park, or if you were bleeding when you bumped your head on the corner cabinet. Pain is a natural warning signal that something is wrong. So is the feeling of emptiness. It is a warning signal that what we are doing is not taking care of the problem.

We try and drown out that wee voice that keeps reminding us that something is missing in a multitude of ways. In fact, the modern human is remarkably inventive at finding ways to squash that inner voice. Technology is our greatest tool and lends itself beautifully to the "bait and switch" mentality we have developed to appease our hunger for more. The computer I am sitting at now is a perfect example. Functional, yes, but also—when hooked to the Internet—one of the greatest playthings devised by humankind. Shopping is another. How many of us have bought things we didn't really need? How many of you remember the pet rock? How many of you still own one? Come on, now. Fess up. After you pay real money for a garden-variety rock, it's kind of hard to just toss it over the fence. I'll bet you still have one in the basement somewhere.

We enlist diversions to tease our attention away from that feeling of emptiness, loneliness, and loss. Shopping, food, extreme sports, sex, television, and the list goes on and on. We can't even enjoy the fruits of our efforts because almost immediately the desire for a bigger and better model worms its way into our brains. We can never fill the abyss of emptiness by trying to load it with things, thoughts, and emotions. That would be like marking out the red oil warning light in your car with a black felt tip marker so you aren't constantly reminded that you are low on oil. Emptiness, boredom, restlessness, and anxiety—like physical pain—are red warning lights. They are trying to tell us that something is wrong. They are telling us that outward activity will not secure inner peace. We have been going outward to gain more and more when the answer lies in the other direction.

So, what is the problem? Why do we feel the unrelenting spur to achieve and acquire more and more? The problem is that we don't need more. We need less. In fact, we need less than less. We need nothing. I know it sounds crazy, but it is true. Here's how it works.

Quantum physics tells us that there are two sides to life: 1) the field of form and energy, and 2) the Nothing that it all comes from. Actually, quantum physics wasn't the first to point this out. Spiritual texts like the Vedas and Upanashads, Taoist and Buddhist scripture and Christian doctrine all refer to the void that existed before creation. So, what's the big deal? It turns out that Nothing is not empty. Now stick with me here; this is where it gets interesting. All the things of creation— star dust and anti-matter and ladybugs and sweet dreams— exist in the relative world of form and energy. Surrounding and interpenetrating the field of form is Nothing. Nothing has all the building blocks to fill our cosmic existence with an infinite multiplicity of things, but as Nothing they have not yet taken form.

How do we know Nothing exists? Well, saints and scientists alike have told us it's there. David Bohm, a quantum mechanical theorist who was referred to by Einstein as his intellectual son, called Nothing "implicate order." The first two verses of Genesis reflect, "In the beginning...the world was without form, and void." The echo of Nothing was also heard over 3,000 years ago in the first line of the Taittiriya Upanishad: "In the beginning, the world was not."

But, Nothing couldn't just sit there so it got busy with the business of creation. Its first activity was thinking. Its first thought was about itself. What else was there to think about? This first thought created the sense of Self, that unbounded essence you know as "I." Then Nothing thought about all the really neat things it could create. That is when

Nothing became something. Genesis further observes, "And the Spirit of God moved upon the waters. And God said, "Let there be light; and there was light." Taittiriya Upanishad also informs us, "From non-existence came Existence. From itself Existence created the Self. Thus, it is called the Self-Made." So you see, this idea of Nothing creating everything has been around for awhile. And there is a reason for that.

When you add the idea if Nothing, along with the experience of Nothing, it has a most remarkable effect on us. It removes suffering. That's right. Nothing eradicates anguish, misery, and distress. It balances disharmony of every kind and invigorates the body and mind alike. It is truly the magic bullet that targets every malady and madness of mankind. And it does so effortlessly, eliminating the need for struggle and strain. One size fits all. So, when the ego goes out to look for fulfillment in a new relationship or a new car, it had better bring along Nothing or it will end up with something it doesn't want: suffering.

Crazy, isn't it? We think we need to gather around us more stuff like wealth and friends to feel complete. But as we all know, anything we can gain, we can lose. We all know people who have lost fortunes and friends that they once thought were theirs for life. It is not the losing that causes suffering. It is, instead, the fear of loss and the longing for its return. Things and people are not the problem. It is the mind's attachment to them that creates the torment. The mind attaches to things because it doesn't know the value of Nothing. If you have Nothing, you have nothing to lose. I think this last statement needs a little explanation.

Let's look at it in terms of peace. When we are peaceful, we are not suffering, are we? Peace and fear cannot coexist. A quiet mind cannot comprehend suffering. They are diametrically opposed. Peace doesn't push out fear and suffering; it just won't allow them to exist in that nurturing atmosphere. Peace is infertile ground for fear. It might serve us well to understand a little more about peace if we are to ever get a handle on suffering.

What is peace? If we look at it as an expression of, more or less, mental activity, we would say that peace is less activity, right? When you feel peaceful, your mind is quiet, isn't it? Think of watching a sunset or sitting on a log in the woods as opposed to having an argument with your boss.

Even if your body is active, you can be at peace. Long-distance runners often talk about having inner peace even while their body is working very hard. The point is that true peace is reflected in the quiet mind no matter what the body is doing.

So, we could say that less and less mental activity reflects more and more peace. If this is so, then we might also be able to say that no activity is absolutely peace. Activity is energy, and no activity is no energy. No energy is Nothing. Therefore, Nothing is absolute peace. Clever, huh?

The ego is always looking to add something to enhance its existence. It feels that more education, better health, or more money will create the peace and freedom from anxiety. The problem is that adding things is adding energy, and adding energy, as we already know, is opposed to peace. This is a very important point. If finding peace were a mathematical process, it would have to involve subtraction, not addition. Take a minute and think about subtracting things from your life. Don't you feel even a little less anxious when you think about not having to go to work or perhaps even not go on vacation? Even good experiences like a vacation can cause stress. How many times have you returned from vacation and felt you could finally get some rest? Well, here is the good news. I have discovered a way that you can keep your active life and still have a quiet mind—just like the runner whose body is very active but his mind is at rest. It will take a little practice, but the results are immediate and inspiring. Once you learn the simple process of Quantum Entrainment (QE), you will be able to effortlessly heal yourself and your friends of the apparent disharmony of daily life.

Mathematically, the QE process works by subtraction. It offers your mind less and less and less until Nothing is left. Then—and this is the really neat part—it holds your mind at that most delicate level of creation, where your inner Self abides, while at the same time allowing it to float gently back to the hustle and bustle of everyday living. You truly have a foot in two worlds, drawing sustenance simultaneously from both. This is your key to unlocking peace and eliminating suffering. See how simple it is? Once you learn this simple two-step process, you will be able to create peace and harmony wherever you go, in whatever you do. You will be able to improve your relationships as well as your emotional and physical health, financial condition, athletic performance, and spiritual pursuits; you will even be able to help others do the same. Now, how incredible is that? Simply by doing Nothing you set in motion healing waves of change that ripple not only within your own life but throughout creation. Are you beginning to see the power and potential of this effortless and most innocent process? (Author's note: It is beyond the spirit and scope of this book to venture too deeply into the fascinating study of the mechanics of life and living. But if you are interested in further exploring these and other ideas like them, then pick up a copy of *Beyond Happiness: How You Can Fulfill Your Deepest Desire*, written by this author.)

I think I have talked about ego and peace and Nothing for long enough. It's time I offered you a chance to experience Nothing so that what I have written above will hold meaning for you. Actually, you won't be experiencing Nothing. Because it can only cognize forms like "thought" and "emotion" and translate what the senses bring to it from the outside world, the mind cannot directly experience Nothing. The mind needs some structure to attach to. Nothing is formless and as you will see (or won't see, actually), Nothing is known by the lack of experience. So, let's get to it, shall we?

CHAPTER 3

Pure Awareness

...anywhere is the center of the world.

Black Elk

No one has seen God and lived.
To see God, we must be nonexistent.

Hazrat Inayat Khan

Have you ever wondered what lies at the bottom of your mind? If you could tap into the source of your thoughts, would it improve your sex life, your health, your ability to love and live free from worry? Where do your thoughts come from, and what possible impact could that knowledge have on your day-to-day, practical life? Let's take a few minutes to explore these questions and see where it leads us.

It turns out that uncovering the source of your thoughts has a definite and overwhelmingly positive influence on personal relations, financial success, physical and emotional fitness, and even your love life. It's simply a matter of slipping the bonds of energy/matter and experiencing what lies beyond. All things are forms of energy. For instance, the chair you may be sitting in has enough energy to effectively suspend your backside 18 inches from the floor for an indefinite period of time. Thoughts are mental energy, sparks of spirit, igniting the mind and everything it touches.

How do we know this? Any created thing—and that includes a

thought—has two qualities. It is both energy and form. For instance, the chair you are sitting in is energy in the form of a chair. You know it has energy because it is holding you up, and energy in that form we agree to call a chair, right? You could call your chair a "capacity support," for instance, and that may lead to all sorts of interesting inquiries, but in the end (pun intended), no matter what we call it, your chair is still a specific energy with a specific form.

Thoughts are not as solid as chairs or hairs or Kodiak bears, but they exist and therefore have form and energy. And being created things, thoughts have to come from somewhere. That somewhere is actually nowhere. That is, the source of thought is the same as the source of all created things that we mentioned above. Thought comes from Bohm's implicate order, the "void," the Nothing.

I'd like to borrow an analogy from Maharishi Mahesh Yogi and liken the mind to a pond. A thought would be like a bubble rising from the bottom of the pond expanding until it bursts on the surface of the pond. The surface of the pond is akin to the conscious level of the mind where we become aware of thought. The bottom of the pond where bubbles come from is likened to the Nothing that gives birth to all created things.

Like bubbles rising toward the surface of a pond, thoughts expand, dispersing their energy and becoming weaker as they rise. The further a thought moves away from its source, the more it exhausts its energy. Thought is the precursor to action. So it is easy to see that weak thought leads to weak and ineffectual action. If we follow this further, we can easily see that if we could become aware of a thought closer to its origin, then we would benefit from more energetic, less distorted thinking. All of us could use a little of that.

Let me ask you this: Have you ever run out of thoughts? I didn't think so. One thing we can say about thoughts is, from our first breath to our last, they are there. If thoughts are energy, and we never run out of them, then it stands to reason that the source of thought is an inexhaustible supply of energy. It also seems that we might benefit greatly if we could directly tap into our source of thought. I am certainly not the first to point this out. Wise men and women have been trying to get us interested in this very exercise for eons. If this were possible, every aspect of our lives would be wonderfully transformed. Hold onto your hats because it is possible!

Now, we can banter about abstract theories and fanciful philosophies until we are blue in the face, but that only strengthens or weakens belief. Experience is the proof of the pudding. My job is to see that you get that experience. So, let's get started.

The Stopping Thought Exercise

Sit comfortably and close your eyes. Now, pay attention to your thoughts. Just follow them wherever they may lead. Simply watch them come and go. After you have watched your thoughts for five to ten seconds, ask yourself the following question, and then wait, in a very alert state to see what happens right after you ask. Here's the question: Where will my next thought come from?

What happened? Was there a short break in your thinking while you waited for the next thought? Did you notice a space, a kind of gap between the question and the next thought? Okay, now reread the instructions, and perform the exercise again. I'll wait...

Did you notice a slight hesitation in your thinking—a pause between thoughts? If you were alert immediately after you asked the question, you will have noticed that your mind was just waiting for something to happen. Author of *The Power of Now*, Eckhart Tolle, says it is like a cat watching a mouse hole. You were awake, waiting, but there were no thoughts in that gap. You may have heard that it takes many years of arduous practice to clear the mind of thoughts, but you have just done it in a matter of seconds.

Please do this exercise again. Do it for 2–3 minutes with eyes closed. Every 15 seconds or so, ask the original question or use substitute questions like, "What color will my next thought be?" or "What will my next thought smell like?" The question is not important, but paying attention is. Watch the gap closely when it is there. Look for it when it is not. Attention will expose the gap—the space between thoughts. *This gap is the source of thought.* It may be fleeting, but it will be there. As you regularly become aware of this mental pause, it will begin to work its magic on you.

OK, now close your eyes and do the Stop Thinking exercise for 2–3 minutes. I'll wait...

Finished? Good. How do you feel right now? Do you feel some relaxation in your body? Are your thoughts quieter? Do you feel stillness or peace? How can this happen? All you did was observe the gap between thought and automatically, without effort, your body became more relaxed and your mind more peaceful. That is what happens when you begin to function and live in the quieter levels of the mind. The body and mind are intimately related and when the mind stops thinking so hard, the body gets to relax and become more rested. You already know how to make the body tense and rigid by becoming mentally stressed. Tight neck and shoulders, headaches, digestive problems, constipation, and hypertension are all manners of physical ailments resulting from a chaotic, runaway mind. You have just discovered how to combat the problem of mental/emotional/physical stress in three minutes. Remarkable, isn't it? This is just the tip of the QE iceberg, but with this simple exercise you can begin to get a feel for the potential of embracing Nothing.

Now, let me ask you this: "When you were observing the gap between your thoughts, were you worried about paying your bills, making dinner, or remembering your spouse's birthday?" Of course not. Your mind was completely still and free of worry. It is impossible to be completely aware of Nothing and suffer from fear, anxiety, remorse, guilt, or any other discordant or destructive emotion. If you did nothing else but learn this forceful lesson, you would be able to dramatically alter your life's course toward more prosperity, creativity, and love. But there is much more.

Let's continue to discover what additional pearls of perception await us from this enlightening exercise. First, tell me what was in the gap? What did you say? A little louder, please...Oh, you said, "Nothing." That's right, there was nothing in the gap. There was no form, sound, color, smell—nothing! Or we could say Nothing was in the gap and be equally correct. Are you beginning to see the magnitude of this simple discovery?

For those of you who thought you were your thoughts and emotions, your memories, hopes, and fears, then maybe you have another thing coming. Thoughts and emotions come and go. They are relative and momentary. You, your essence is so much more than your mind can even dream, and you just proved it.

When your thinking stopped, did you cease to exist? Did you go into a coma or somehow become unconscious or unaware? Of course not. You were still there, weren't you? Well, if you aren't your thoughts and you were still there, then who are you? That seems like a fair question, doesn't it? If you don't know who you are, then everything you do is baseless, without foundation. You become like a man with amnesia who is trying to live his life but doesn't really know who he is. To plant your feet firmly on the foundation of life, you must know who you are. And I can guarantee that you are not foremost a person with a past and future. You will be surprised to discover that you are, in fact, unbounded and beyond time and trouble.

Let's take a closer look to see how you are beyond time and trouble. In the gap between thought, there was Nothing. But you were still aware. You were watching when the thoughts first disappeared and were replaced by the gap. But who was watching the gap?

Now, let's see. Nothing was there, but you were still aware. There was nothing there but awareness. Not awareness of something but a pure awareness of Nothing. Do you have it? Do you see where we are headed? If there was nothing there but pure awareness, then you must necessarily be that pure awareness. What else could you be?

If your awareness identifies with your thoughts, your memories, and your future plans, you are referring to the "me." "Me" is the collected "things" of your life. "Me" is your age, your sex, your likes and loves, and your memories. But none of that exists at the moment your awareness turns inward and observes the gap between thoughts. To observe, you must be aware, right? So, at that moment when your mind turned off, you were aware of the nothing we call Nothing. But you found out that Nothing is not empty. Nothing is filled with pure awareness. And now you have solved the mystery of who you are. *You are pure awareness!*

Does that sound impossible? The fact cannot be denied. Your direct perception has revealed you to be pure awareness. That's right. Before "me" was born and built into the image you recognize as yourself, there was the solitary, universal Nothing of pure awareness. Stop and ponder the profundity of this realization for a moment...I'll wait.

Are you awed at your own immensity? Are you getting a feel for your boundless, ever-present nature? Liberating, isn't it?

Let's think on this a little longer. Remember a time when you were a child. Now, stop to look at a time during your adolescence, young adulthood, and the present. At each stage of your life, you had different likes, desires, and goals. Your body, mind, and emotions also changed. In fact, Nothing stayed the same. What has remained unchanged from childhood through adulthood? It is your awareness. At each stage of your life—no, each second of your life—while your body/mind was busy becoming what it is today, you, pure awareness, stood silent vigil, a timeless witness.

Through the Stopping Thought exercise you were able to "go inside" as it were and watch your thinking. Then, while waiting ("Like a cat watching a mouse hole"), you observed the gap between thought. You recognized the gap to be pure awareness and pure awareness to be your unbound essence—the foundation upon which the "me" part of you rests. If you, pure awareness, is truly unbounded, then you are not limited to your mind. You, pure awareness, should be everywhere, all the time, shouldn't you? As it turns out, you are, and here is a simple exercise that you can do to prove it to your "me."

The Hand-to-Hand Exercise

Hold your arms out fully extended and to your sides so you form a human cross. Look at the back of your right hand. Note what it looks like for 3–5 seconds. Now turn your head to the left to look at the back of your left hand. Now tell me, what was in your mind during the time that you looked from your right hand to your left? Nothing, right? You were not unaware during that time, were you? Of course not. There was a gap in your thinking while your eyes shifted from hand to hand, but your awareness remained turned on. Do it again. See! Even when your mind is turned outward into the world, it will still find pure awareness. Pure awareness is always there underlying everything, just waiting to be discovered; waiting for "me" to become aware of you, pure awareness.

Let's not forget awareness is not an object. It is you, your unbounded essence. Your mind will not be able to completely accept this because it can't conceive of Nothing. There must be a boundary, some form for your mind to latch onto so it can do what minds must do—experience, record, analyze, synthesize, and compartmentalize information. It is the ego that decides what to do with this information. So don't feel concerned if you keep identifying with your body/mind in the beginning. This is the only option your mind has, and it takes time for the ego to move aside and accept boundless pure awareness as the ultimate reality and your primal essence.

Why is revealing this truth so absolutely vital? When you come to know yourself as unchanging, unbounded, eternal awareness, your dependence on the withering body and failing mind begins to loosen its hold. You become aware that you are beyond the field of change and death. You become aware that, beyond all the things and thoughts that "me" is, you remain fully unbroken and aware.

If just a few minutes of observing the gap between your thoughts brought peace and relaxation, imagine what joyful adventures await you when pure awareness infuses your thinking, eating, working, and loving. Discovering pure awareness at the bottom of your mind and vibrating outward through the simplicity of atoms to the symphony of the spheres is the first step to living a full and bounteous life. Teasing it out to support and nurture your every activity is the next step.

CHAPTER 4

I Thought I Thought
the Thought I Thought

You cannot possibly say that you are what you think
yourself to be! To know what you are, you must first
investigate and know what you are not.

Nisargadatta

When thought struggles against the results, trying to avoid
those unpleasant results while keeping on with that way of
thinking. That is what I call 'sustained incoherence'.

David Bohm

As far as the mind is concerned, this gap between thoughts is not much to write home about. It is just a space filled with silence, obvious only after one thought goes and before the next thought appears. Looking back on the experience, your mind doesn't find it very interesting. Your mind loves movement and form. The gap is free of both. It contains Nothing. Nothing means, well, nothing to the mind. But that is a big mistake. And here is why. All the thoughts in the mind come from that nothing. Test it for yourself. Repeat the Stopping Thought exercise and watch the gap. Automatically, and without any effort on your part, the next thought spontaneously arrives. There it is, bright as day—a brand new thought. That's pretty miraculous

31

when you stop to think about it (pun intended). Each new thought is a marvel of creation, and it comes from Nothing. So Nothing must not be empty. There must be something in that Nothing; otherwise, it could not produce a thought. Interesting, isn't it?

One more time, perform the Stopping Thought exercise for a minute or so. I'll wait...

You were aware of the gap, right? While you were "in the gap" there was no thinking going on. Then after some time, thoughts started up again, didn't they? Now, while you were in the gap, did you say, "Hey, I'm just hanging out doing nothing. I think I'll start thinking again"? Then did you decide what your next thought would be? Of course you didn't. Thoughts just started up again all by themselves. And that thought could have been about the gap or your Aunt Tillie's mustache. There is just no knowing what we will be thinking about because we have no say over the matter. Our ego-oriented "me" has been taking credit for thinking for as long as we can remember. But it just isn't true. You have as much influence over your life—including your thoughts, hopes, fears, and loves—as someone watching a movie has over the characters reflected on the screen.

You will have the same "not in control" experience if you do the "hand-to-hand" exercise. When you shift your attention from the back of one hand to the other there is only pure awareness reflecting in your mind. You might ask, "How were my eyes guided to the second hand if nothing was going on in my mind?" Or, "How did I know when to stop?" These are disturbing questions if you believe "me" is doing the thinking. It is also disturbing to think that pure awareness is in control because that puts you, your ego, totally out of the picture.

The "me" does not produce thought. We don't think thoughts. Thoughts arrive spontaneously out of pure awareness. The ego does not produce thought, but it takes all the credit for thinking. A thought appears on the scene without any great fanfare. It is born of silence and moves effortlessly in the quiet depths of the mind. If we become aware of a thought as it is born, then we appreciate it as a creation of pure awareness. If our awareness is anchored outward toward the tumultuous turmoil of sensory existence, it misses the creation of this delicate spark of life. Such an unaware mind picks up a thought far away from the stillness that gave it life. This mind, when it is aware of thought, appreciates only its active and agitated form. This mind is ever striving to control its can-of-worms desires, never finding rest. Awareness of a thought at its conception takes place in a confident and quiet mind completely at ease with its roll as witness to creation.

The further away from its conception a thought is realized, the more weakened and distorted it becomes and the more trouble it gets into. Every erratic thought implores us to turn inward and become aware of the autonomy of thought at its very point of origin. We have been lazy in this regard and it has gotten us in a real pickle. You only have to look around at the present state of our world to know we are not living anywhere near our potential. The symptoms of egocentric living are overwhelming and will overwhelm us completely in the end. Our only salvation is, as it has always been, to overcome authorship of thought. By doing so, we hand the burden of thinking and all that goes with it over to pure awareness.

I know this idea of not being in control of your thinking is a little hard to accept, but once you are able to let go of that belief, you will experience a great weight lifted from your shoulders. I'd like to spend a few minutes taking a deeper look at this possibility. I would like you to see for yourself the beautifully simple realization of life beyond effort or control. Most of us feel we have mastered control over our thinking. That is, we can choose and direct our thinking as we like. That is a grand illusion more easily maintained by the ego looking at the sheer volume of thoughts and saying, "They are all mine. I don't have to prove it because everyone knows that it is true." If you are, indeed, the master of all your thoughts, then you should be able to exert control over one single, lowly thought, shouldn't you? Let's see.

Wherever you are at this moment, think only one thought for one minute. That's right, for one full minute, eliminate all other thoughts except the one you have chosen. For instance, think the thought "tree" for 60 seconds. Were you able to effortlessly hold your mind still on that single thought without wandering for a minute? You probably could not do it without another thought slipping in for more than a few seconds. It requires great effort to go against the natural flow of thought from pure awareness. And did you notice how easily other thoughts slipped into your consciousness? In this case, struggle is a sign that you are swimming upstream against the natural flow of life. But we have been taught otherwise. How can we know when we are in the flow and when we are creating disharmony? Let's look a little more deeply into this question.

Let's start at the very beginning. We have no control over who we are. We had no control over who our parents were, nor over which sperm fertilized which of our mother's eggs. Did we oversee the construction of our bodies as the miracle of us unfolded cell by cell? At birth were we able to choose the environmental forces, the climate (both physical and emotional), the food we were fed, our siblings, and so on that would shape the new born "me"? We have been pretty much at the mercy of our genetic hardwiring and unique environmental forces that have molded and tempered us into the individuals we are today.

When we take a broader view, we can see that we are reflexively reactive. Even our current thoughts are in reaction to thoughts, conditions, and stimuli that preceded them. Contemplating the solution to a complex problem is still only reacting to a previous line of thinking with another thought. How we react is completely dependant on our genetic disposition and environmental imprinting. If I had exactly the same genes and environmental structuring as you, I would be you. I would have no other choice, right? Being you in every way, I would have to act and react just like you. Where would my choice to be different come in? You see, we do not have the control we thought we had. It is the grand illusion that feeds ego and keeps us chained to the cause and effect "wheel of karma."

Karl Renz, in his book *The Myth of Enlightenment*, puts it this way, "Simply see that any contribution you made always happened on its own. It operated on its own and didn't need your decision. You fear that, without your decision, nothing would happen, but that's just an idea." He goes on to say, "Nothing depends on you...Every idea is spontaneous, every apparent decision comes out of nothing, out of the blue, from the great beyond."

Let's look at it from another angle. When has anything worked out exactly as you planned? I said *exactly*, not generally. Sure, you can say, "I wanted a new house and I have it." But I can guarantee you that specific plans were continually thwarted along the way—things such as unexpected bills, trouble with the bank, unexpected inheritance, illness, and so on. Your life *never* works the way you plan for it to; sometimes it works out for the better, other times for the worse.

Let's say you meet someone new and desire to spend your life together. Based on what you have shared and learned about them, you have a pretty good idea of how your life will unfold together, right? You have plans and hopes of how your life will play out over the next few months, years, and decades. But has any relationship ever worked out even close to what you had wanted or expected? I think not. In fact, if you want to smooth the rocky ride of relationships, the best thing you can do is to sit back and let the relationship take its own course. Micromanaging, knit-picking, and nagging only makes things worse. Oddly, it is in the letting go that we get. Effort and control are contrary to fulfillment and peace.

So, what's the point? What value is there in challenging ego and establishing a concept that is so foreign as to be ludicrous? When we realize and accept that we are even a little less in control of what we think and do, we find that peace starts to get a grip on our mind. Every impulse to be in command has as its ultimate goal: inner peace. Fighting to keep control keeps us flailing around on the surface of our minds like a drowning man awash in an ocean of colliding forces. Paradoxically, when we stop struggling and let go, we do not drown. True, we sink to the silent depths of our ocean-like minds. There, in the non-moving profundity of complete stillness, we are astonished to find that everything is permeated by pure awareness. There we find perfect harmony devoid of even the impulse of effort. Nisargadatta, one of my favorite

20th century saints, describes how he found freedom from control in his book *I Am That*. To one seeker who approached him the desire to remove inner strife he lovingly imparted, "While the mind is centered in the body and consciousness is centered in the mind, awareness is free. By looking tirelessly, I became quite empty and with that emptiness, all came back to me except the mind. I find I have lost the mind irretrievably."

This is the goal of Quantum Entrainment (QE). QE entertains the mind and satisfies the needs of the ego while simultaneously showing it that effort is not needed to get what we want. In fact, effort makes any task harder than it needs to be. It is a hindrance to the outward flow of creativity and the inner knowing of personal peace. In time, as one plays with the infinite possibilities of QE, the lesson of effortlessness slowly integrates itself into our thinking, our actions, and our interactions with those around us.

When we begin to live life free of the desire to control, we not only have inner peace, the goal of all desire, but we are rewarded outwardly in a way that defies conventional thinking. When the desire for things begins to die, we are given those very things without asking and without effort on our part. These gifts are not sought, and that increases the joy of receiving them. It also fosters humility and a sense awe for the perfect harmony of pure awareness and its manifestations. Any idea of control is as out of place as a frat party in a monastery, and about as welcome.

The following is an excerpt from *Beyond Happiness*.

> To ask why things are the way they are reflects a desire to see beyond your slice of life, and know the primal mind and ultimate makeup of the universe. Somehow we feel that if we can understand the cosmic mind, we will then understand our own. From there it should be a short leap to fixing the wrongs of our life and then we can live in peace and harmony. While a noble undertaking, it is completely fruitless and still adds up to nothing more than ego's influence born of the need to collect

enough pieces to make one whole. But you don't need to do that. The phrase, "If it ain't broke, don't fix it" comes to mind. If we feel incomplete, we try and fix the perceived problem. The cosmic joke is on us, the thinking species. It is only the thought that we are not whole that makes us feel that we are not. When we let go of that thought, we immediately realize that everything is just as it should be. You are already whole, not because I say so but because that is the fact. How could any product of Wholeness not be whole? Which is more likely—you are the incomplete product of the complete Creator or you just haven't realized your connection to that unbounded Fullness? There is no why or how to be answered. Everything in this wide beautiful universe is what it is, just because it is, nothing more. There is no arguing with what is. How can you say that what is, is not? Have you put peace in your pocket so that you can have both hands free to rummage through thoughts and things looking for peace? The only thing that stands between you and peace is the thought that life needs fixing. Accept that life is what it is and you give up the struggle to make it otherwise. What takes the place of struggle is peace. That is it. End of story. End of suffering.

Realizing that thought is beyond the influence of "me" is to surrender to what is. This surrender requires awareness of pure awareness, allowing that pure awareness to be in control. Actually, that is not at all true. Pure awareness, by its very nature, can't be in control. We have been discussing the two worlds; absolute pure awareness and the rest of creation. In actuality, there is only one unmoving, indivisible, whole, pure awareness, which appears as many. We cannot give anything to pure awareness. Pure awareness just is. It is everywhere, all the time and therefore cannot get or give anything. Because of the limitations of language, we will sally forth as if pure awareness could be separated from our minds. This will foster the illusion of turning inward to heal outwardly and that is OK, for those are the rules of the game. Soon, by practicing QE, we will learn to split ourselves, one half playing, while the other quietly watches. In time, the two halves will reunite and heal in full awareness, and life will be at once mundane and awe inspiring. In our palm an ordinary stone will sing the siren song of deep and lasting peace. Then our world will contain not a blemish of disharmony, and we will be at last free.

CHAPTER 5

Getting to Know Your Self

This thing called the Way - where does it exist?

Tung-kuo Tzu

All truth passes through three stages.
First, it is ridiculed. Second, it is violently opposed.
Third, it is accepted as being self-evident.

Arthur Schopenhauer

Socrates, by most accounts, was a pretty sharp fellow. He is credited with saying, "Know thy Self." Many of my professors translated this as "Know thyself." That is the little self of id, ego, and super-ego, the "me" previously mentioned, collecting kids, a mortgage, and retirement plan. But this is not our concern today as we have a bigger fish to fry. We are going to discover our big Self and explore its place in the universe. You might ask why we would want to do that. Why did Socrates feel it important? What possible benefits would befall us if we become chummy with our big Self? And, what the heck is our Self anyway? Let's take a look.

If our ego-oriented mind does not create thought, and pure awareness does not create thought, then who or what does? That would be our Self. Our Self is unique in all creation. It has a foot in both worlds—the absolute sea of pure awareness and the multi-splintered expressions of the created cosmos.

39

Quantum physics has several names for Self. It can be likened to the zero point or the vacuum state but shouldn't be confused it with implicate order. Implicate order is analogous to pure awareness. If your interest goes any deeper than this then I encourage you to do a little research on your own for we will not spend further time on this fascinating, but altogether too vast a subject for our purposes. The point is that both the Self and pure awareness have been recognized theoretically by quantum physics.

The Self has also been recognized by those who turn inward within the mind—the saints and seekers of inner peace. They have called the Self by many names including spirit, divine spark, higher Self, vital force, and soul. I do not use these words for they are fraught with misunderstanding and laden with emotional charge. Knowing thy Self, as you will soon see, is the most natural, delicate, and nurturing experience a human can have. So I don't want to get all balled up in intellectual or emotional wrestling matches. Our Self is simple and so will be our discussion of it. Simpler yet will be our experience of Self just a short chapter away. Awareness of our Self is the birthright of every human being. It is also my strong opinion that becoming aware of our Self is our greatest responsibility.

I think the best way to get a handle on understanding your Self is with an analogy. We'll start with an updated version of Plato's Cave. Picture yourself sitting in a movie theatre while the movie is playing. You are looking forward as the film flows across the vast white screen. You don't notice the screen because you are focused on the characters, the scenery, and the plot as they totally draw you into the experience. When you become completely absorbed in the intrigue of the unfolding story, you become less aware of your surroundings. That is as it should be. After all, that's why we go to movies—to get away from the "reality" of our day-to-day lives.

But if I were to ask you to shift your attention away from the film, you could become aware of many things surrounding you in the audience. You might become aware of a cough in the back row, the munching, slurping, and rustling from your immediate neighbors, and many other stimuli like the firmness of your seat, room temperature, etc. But I would like you now to focus on less common objects.

When you arrive before the movie starts, you note with absolute certainty the mammoth size of the white screen, a mute testimony to the bigger-than-life entertainment just ahead. As soon as the movie starts, the screen is completely forsaken for the play of light and shadow upon it. If you sit in the first couple of rows and you don't let your eye follow the movement of your favorite hero as he rolls across the floor to avoid being ventilated by bullets from the villain's Uzi, you will see that the screen is still there, behind the scenes silently supporting your hero's efforts. Without it, the movie would be lost in the vastness of space.

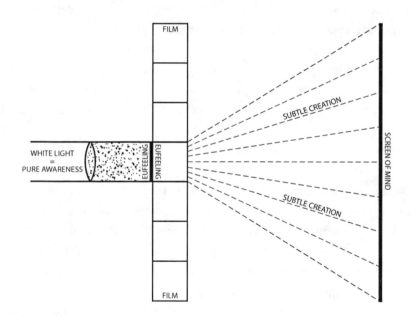

Now, break with convention and turn around and look at the little square hole high up the back wall of the theatre. There you can see a white shaft of light, sometimes tinged with blue and black hues, twisting and flicking on its way to the screen in front. If you are positioned just right you will see the lens of the projector and behind that the pure, bright light that brings the film to life.

Obviously the playing of the film on the screen symbolizes the comedy and drama of your own work-a-day world. The blank screen upon which the film is played represents the screen of pure awareness such as you experienced when you stopped your thinking just a short time ago. Stopping your thinking is analogous to stopping the movie and allowing the white light to fall on the blank screen. The screen represents the reflection of pure awareness in the mind. Pure awareness, when reflecting outward in the mind, I call consciousness. Consciousness is awareness directed at things and thoughts. If you had always entered the theatre after the movie had started and had never seen the blank screen, it would be almost impossible to discover the white screen under the colorful, moving forms cast upon it.

Now once again, turn around to look at the light as it exits the back wall. The shifting, flickering shaft of light represents the finer levels of creation beyond the sensory. This light represents the waves, particles, atoms, and molecules that finally weave their way into form on the surface of the screen.

Emanating from the projector, before it passes through the film, is the "Self-Made" white light. It is this white light passing through the film and projecting its images onto the screen that makes the movie possible. We could not be conscious of the screen itself without reflected white light. The creation of the movie depends solely on this white light. The white light represents unbounded pure awareness.

When the white light passes through the film, it apparently changes into color, light, and shadow. I say apparently because it is still light but it appears to the eye to be otherwise. Refracted white light is still light at its essence. This analogy will help us better understand how pure awareness can manifest as those things around us which appear to be houses, mountains, friends, and family. A mountain is made of molecules, atoms, subatomic particles, and waves, which are refractions of the implicate order of pure awareness. The white light is to the movie as pure awareness is to all created things. It is their essence, their very core, without which they would fade into the beckoning void of Nothing.

At the point that the white light of the projector strikes the film is where this apparent transformation takes place. Like a pencil placed in a half-full glass of water appears to be bent, the white light of the projector passes through the film, taking on altered vibrational qualities. At the exact point of transformation, a rather miraculous event occurs. The white light and its color manifestation are held in suspension. They are neither white light nor color. Or they are both at the same time. Like the back and forth movement of a child on a swing, there is a time when she is neither moving backwards nor forwards but is suspended motionless in mid-air. This is the rejuvenating power of stillness that we know between each heartbeat and each breath. White light enters this sphere of stillness and exits color. This is where creation takes place—between pure awareness and the first impulse of created life. This is the realm of the Self.

This reflection of awareness in the mind is called consciousness or focused awareness. The shaft of flickering light that the white light makes as it passes through the film on its way to the screen would be analogous to consciousness. Consciousness is forever changing but it is fundamentally white light. Outward-oriented consciousness is ego driven. It takes ownership for thoughts and deeds alike. It is restless and rarely content. It is like the beam of a flashlight, and ego is the hand that is holding it. It shines on all the things of the world and fails to realize that without the light of pure awareness from which it is made, consciousness cannot fully appreciate the eternal nature of a budding rose or flowing stream. Consciousness is looking for pure awareness in the things and thoughts of the relative world. It is like the man in the Waylon Jennings song who is "looking for love in all the wrong places."

All the beauty, variety, and excitement of the world splashes across the screen of your mind as consciousness flickers outward. But when your conscious mind turns back on itself, as it did in the Stopping Thought exercise, it realizes its true nature as pure awareness. This would be like the ego-aimed flashlight pointing at a mirror. The true nature of your consciousness, the dazzling radiance of pure awareness could be seen in its naked beauty without the distraction of form.

It is impossible for our minds to understand either pure awareness or our Self. An idea is really a hollow reverberation of the truth of Self. But we will have to be satisfied for now with this house of straw the mind has built. In the end, it really doesn't matter how we think about Self for it is the experience of that universally unique presence that will open our minds and hearts to healing and harmony in our lives.

Before we go on and experience our Self, I would like to explore more about what Self is like. Self is unlike anything else in creation. It is the only manifestation that is totally harmless and completely nurturing. To my mind, the perfect word for Self is Mother—unbounded love, wisdom, and support. Mother Self is always there sustaining and guiding you even when your attention is turned to the more mundane matters of daily living. She has created this vast world for you to play in. She is watching, waiting for you to grow, not in body and mind but in awareness. She is waiting for you to turn from your toys to find her benevolent smile and sparkling eyes watching over you. She is waiting to enfold you in arms of pure awareness.

You are the child of your Self when you are lost in the world. But the moment you become aware of your Self, you become your Self. You reenter the womb of Mother and are born anew into undying awareness of pure love and peace and joy. It is your responsibility to "know thy Self" and become free of the fetters of outward living. Free from the restrictions of your ego-driven mind, Self-awareness lightens the load of living. In fact, your feet barely touch the ground.

Another word for Self-aware is "enlightenment," but again I hesitate to use this word because it has been explained in so many different ways from so many different teachings and burdened with so many conflicting emotions that I seldom refer to it at all. It is my intention to clearly define Self-awareness and what it is to live Self-aware so that there will be little room for misinterpretation. Why do I insist on so precise a definition? How else will you know where you are headed or even if you want to go there? Besides, being Self-aware is the foundation for a productive, prosperous, fun-filled life and the heart around which

Quantum Entrainment (QE) orbits. Knowledge comes in two packages—understanding and experience. First, we will gather in the pieces to be learned about Self-awareness. Once they form a cogent whole, we will then fly on the gossamer wings of Self-awareness, observing our world from the inside out.

Living in Self-awareness is not at all what we usually think it to be. We listen to the words of the sages and it sounds like heaven on earth. It is, but we tend to accent the "heaven" and deny the "earth" part of the equation. We get the feeling that our every desire is immediately fulfilled. Well, it is, but again, not the way we think. Here's what I mean.

Let's say that you are living in ignorance of your Self. That puts you in the 99.9 percentile of the human race. That is the world you seek to flee because of the pain and suffering you feel. Your suffering mind turns away from the hardness of the world toward the illusion of salvation. It takes up overeating, extreme physical activity, drugs, sex, television, and any number of the myriad diversions meant to deflect our consciousness from what we have come to know as stark reality. But as you have come to realize, deflection does not work.

The world out there is not the problem. Your problems are not the problem. Inability to be aware of pure awareness is the problem, and you will soon learn how to solve it. Once you discover how to be Self-aware, what will your world be like? How will you change in relation to your world? I think you will be surprised.

When you realize that life has a mind of its own and you are pretty much along for the ride, you can relax and, as the old Greyhound commercial promised, "leave the driving to us." Us is actually Self. As a passenger, the scenery is the same but now you can enjoy it fully with no concern for direction-finding or getting snarled in traffic. You are on holiday even when you are hard at work in the office.

Symptoms of Sainthood

How will you act when you are Self-aware? You will act just about the same way you acted before. You may be a little more loving, kinder, and easygoing, but don't expect to become something you are not. You will still be you, only more so. You will be free to be the real you and not be worried about doing what others think you should do. You will perform (and this is a biggie) spontaneous right action. That's right; you can do no wrong. Because your self is at the seat of creation, it knows how things are working out, and you will instinctively act in your—and all other's—best interest. That does not mean that others will necessarily agree with your actions, but then they will be looking through the distorted lens of ego, following the road of self-preservation. They see rights and wrongs everywhere. It is what they do because they break the world into helpful and hurtful pieces, people, and events. But through your Self-aware eyes, you see only harmony. How, with such vision, could you do anything wrong? The universe will not allow it.

Be careful not to place Self on a pedestal. It doesn't like it there separated from the rest of creation. Creation is of the Self and It loves Its creation. You see, we don't have to change what is; we only have to appreciate it. Suffering starts when we try to change or deny what is. The gift of your Self is the ability to see perfection in the mundane present.

Will we be "saintly" when we are Self-aware? The idea we have of the saintly saint is a bit of a misnomer. By the way, all saints are Self-aware by definition. So, when you become Self-aware, you will be a saint whether anybody else knows it or not. Chances are, they will not.

The Self-aware come in all shapes and sizes. I know of people who were settled in the Self who were also grumpy, unhealthy, and overweight. The Self-aware love to eat, make love, make money, drive cars, play practical jokes, and watch television. In short, they are just like the unaware with this simple and succinct difference; they are totally accepting of life just as it is.

That means that the unaware will miss the blessing that is you because you are dressed in a plain brown wrapper with no bow. I know this description breaks with the traditional idea of the soft-spoken, slow moving benevolent saint, with the cherub smile, luminescent eyes, and soft, wisdom-laden speech. Most saints travel through life unnoticed because we are looking for an ideal, something they are not. We are looking for *enlightenment* because we think that once we achieve enlightenment, we will rise above the huddled, struggling masses and deliver us smack-dab in the middle of heaven. Sorry, Charlie. The soft-spoken saint was soft-spoken before she became Self-aware. It is blasphemy to think of our saints as being irritable or passing gas like the rest of humanity. The ideal of the saintly saint is just another effort by ego to place something so far out of reach so as to be unattainable or, if attained place us in a special class above other human beings. Ego has had its day and now it is time for it to expand to accept its inheritance as unbounded witness to the wonders of creation.

There is a downside to placing the enlightened above us. It is a practice that frustrates the seeker who tries to emulate the actions of those unique souls in hopes of becoming like them. The gentle ones are not different from their more active, noisy Self-aware peers. But we have turned away from the latter to embrace the former ideal as the poster child for enlightenment. Both types, indeed all Self-aware, are acting in accordance with their genetic makeup molded by the influence of their surroundings. Those of us still struggling with our identity would do well to remember this and leave our preconceived ideas about enlightenment by the side of the road. It is not for their benefit but our own. Believe me, the Self-aware will hardly notice.

Being Self-aware is a human experience, the birthright of every one of us. It should be a common experience—not one that is placed on a pedestal beyond the reach of all but a few dedicated, if not stubborn, spiritual aspirants. It is the common soul that will make Self-awareness a common occurrence in the coming decade, not out of some super-human dedication to the struggle to be free but by simply and effortlessly turning toward pure awareness. We have that effortless technology in the form of QE. As you will soon see, anyone who is conscious can do it simply by following that conscious awareness back to its source.

Self-aware Tony Parsons seconds this sentiment of the common saint. In his book *Invitation to Awaken*, he advises, "We should drop any fixed ideas we have about enlightenment, such as the illusory belief that it brings total goodness, bliss, and purity. Life simply goes on. Occasionally, I may get angry, feel anxiety...When the contraction passes, I quickly return to an all-encompassing acceptance in which the sense of separateness drops away."

So how does it feel to be Self-aware? You will still feel anger, anxiety, and all the other emotions that make you human. The saint is still basically human. Actually, you will be more "human" after you become the silent sentinel of creation. Your body/mind is bound by the same laws as it was before. You will feel everything you felt before, but you will accept those feelings unconditionally as a natural expression of life beyond your control.

What about the fear of death? I personally haven't died only to become my own ghost writer so I can't say for certainty what it is like to die. Viewing past lives is no help either. That phenomenon is observed with detachment and has no substantial value when dealing with corporal flesh and blood. But I know how my perception has changed since I have become conversant with Self. I used to fight aging and illness and deny my mortality. Now the thought of death is oddly comforting. As I age and the reality of losing my body/mind becomes more palpable (and many maintain that I am halfway there for they are certain I have already lost my mind), I observe those symptoms of aging with a kind of curious detachment or even fondness for a natural process that all life innately understands. All saints, when it is their time, succumb to the laws governing physical death. But a saint is not attached to his body/mind in a way losing them will cause suffering. It's like returning home after a walk on a wintry day and slipping off an old overcoat for the last time. Your awareness then easily turns to the warmth of your inner abode and the overcoat is simply forgotten.

That does bring up questions about being injured. When you are Self-aware, can someone cause you pain? It is obvious that you will feel *physical* pain, but what about psychological pain? Can you feel *psychological* pain when settled in the Self?

Remember we said that the saint is still human, right? The Self-aware carry around the thin shell of "me." That is why the saint will pass for a normal, everyday guy to the unaware. They cannot see past the shell into the soul of the saint. In Sanskrit—the ancient language of the

Vedas, sacred Indian texts dating back 4,000 years—the term for this shell of "me" is "laish avidya." While the essence of the saint remains aloof, his body/mind is subservient to the same laws that govern the uninitiated. The shell of "me" can feel hurt. It can feel anger, sadness, disappointment, and the like. This shell is like a plastic bell. When it is struck by the words and deeds of man, its reverberations are weak and muffled and cannot arouse the stronger passions of revenge or greed or guilt. Yes, the enlightened can feel momentary hurt, but this pain is muffled in a blanket of bliss that is the Self. No lasting pain can reach into the depths of a heart bathed in pure awareness.

One of the participants in my QE Master's Workshop had a sister who was a driver for the Dalai Lama. One day she was holding the car door open for the Dalai Lama, and as he stood up, he looked gently into her eyes.

He asked, "You would like to ask me a question?"

She whispered, "Yes, sir, but we are not allowed to talk to you."

He responded graciously, "But you can ask me this question that is in your heart."

She then asked, "Do you ever get angry?"

The Dalai Lama chuckled softly and said, "Of course I do. I am human. I just don't stay angry very long."

The Self-aware shell of "me" can be hurt, but it only serves to wake you momentarily to the realization that you are still functioning through a body/mind that is subservient to all laws, natural and man-made. You will feel anger and anxiety and all manner of desires. But they are only flavors in the wine and will not linger long. They wake you to the joy and the depth of what it is to be completely human.

When you know this world as perfect, then hurtful words and wrongful deeds are recognized as part of that perfection. That realization alone soothes the soul and makes retaliation impossible. How is it possible to rise up against perfection? Any event or action will necessarily be perfect beyond our individual and limited perspective. We are saved from performing or receiving injury. Our egos are at peace.

How long does it take to become Self-aware? The short answer is,

"You are already Self-aware. You just aren't aware of it." But that's not very helpful and can even be frustrating, so let's appease the mind and play in the river of time.

Some souls just pop into Self-awareness. They go to bed in ignorance and awaken awakened. Ramana Maharishi, who many feel was the 20th centuries' greatest saint, fell into a swoon in which he felt he was going to die. He passed out and when he regained consciousness, he was unbounded consciousness. Eckhart Tolle tells a similar story about how he, filled with fear, passed out and awoke free of fear and full of bliss. These individuals are the exception rather than the rule. Most Self-aware souls seem to take their time getting there. It would not be fair to leave you with the impression that the inner light instantly turns on for all of us. Unlike Tom Baudette of Motel 6 fame, we cannot just "leave the light on for you." In most cases, the light of Self-awareness is attached to a dimmer switch that slowly gets brighter over apparent time. I have to say that this is an illusion but one that we should address for those of us who are caught in the "neither fish nor fowl" world between all-out ignorance and being fully Self-aware.

I personally was stuck in a kind of limbo for many years. I'll describe it here for you because you may be experiencing the same thing. Actually, "stuck" is not really the right word. All the while you are in this desert world, you feel stuck but in actuality are becoming aware of pure awareness very quickly. Here is what I mean.

When I was a young man, I was confident that if I worked hard and did all the right things, I would eventually get what I wanted and live happily ever after. I'm talking about replicating the lives of great athletes, business, political, and scientific minds, educators, and entertainers. Of course, like everyone else on this path, I was met with frequent failure and disappointment and had to continually convince myself that other people had achieved "forever after" happiness and so could I. I felt that my parents, teachers, and friends all couldn't be wrong. As I young child, I wanted to be a firefighter in the worst way. One day when I was five, I actually got to ride a fire engine as part of a celebration. We went really, really fast with siren howling and bell clanging and I had my head out the window feeling the wind against my face while looking for the imaginary burning building. That night, as a result of the wind blowing in my ear, I got the worst earache I'd ever experienced, and the next day I decided I really wanted to be a farmer and milk cows and grow stuff slowly and quietly.

Early on in our lives, we think big: professional football player, astronaut, movie star. But as we age and find that these things are not always realistic, we lower our aim a little. When we oil our six-shooter and pack our saddlebags on our way to become a cowboy, we are discouraged by cooler, more experienced minds drawing from a deep reservoir of practical experience. They are certain that we would really be better off to consider accounting, perhaps specializing in cowboy tax returns. Soon we buy into the idea that we will become practical. Then we decide that all that is really important is to make enough money to ensure a great retirement so that we can live happily ever after.

The thing is that every one of us has a place in this perfect plan. We have unique talents and skills, and if we don't use them, we feel something is missing—that something is not quite right. If we yield to convention, the dissatisfaction grows until it manifests as physical or emotional discord. We get sick and we inject that illness into our world.

We are like conductors of electricity—like light bulbs. If the electricity passes through us without resistance, we shine bright and long. Just the slightest interference with the natural flow of electrons will cause more heat and less light. Pure awareness is our electricity. Most of the world's population are poor conductors of pure awareness and necessarily create struggle and strife, not only for themselves but all of us. How many times have you seen people make the same mistake time and time again and not learn from their mistakes? Why does an abused wife stay with her husband? Why do we continue using fossil fuels when we have the technology to be free of them? At present, disharmony far outweighs clear thinking and supportive action in this world. The simple reason is that we are disconnected. We lack the free flow of awareness of pure awareness.

To follow through with our light bulb analogy, those of us unaware of pure awareness are like incandescent light bulbs. We spread a little light over a wide spectrum of wavelengths while wasting much of our energy as heat. In short, we are incoherent expressions of the infinite order in life.

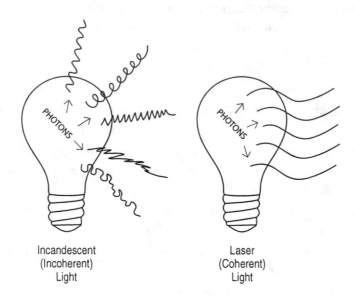

Incandescent
(Incoherent)
Light

Laser
(Coherent)
Light

Those who are aware of pure awareness are like laser light. A laser's light is coherent. That is, all of the photons are in harmony with one another. Instead of shooting off in all directions at all speeds, laser light's photons are completely in sync, like an army marching in time. They are of single mind and remarkably powerful action. Our laser-like awareness is finely focused and completely in tune with Self and environment. The Self-aware engender harmony without harm.

As a child, I, like any healthy youngster, was relatively happy, interactive, and eager to explore my environment. But by age ten, I had begun to succumb to the practical voices of my parents and teachers. I began to enjoy learning how to control through knowledge and power and was applauded when I showed promise. Yup, this was going to be a good life, and I was going to get all the things I wanted through hard work, strong will, and force. I had not yet seen that the very people who had promised me the good life were struggling to find it themselves.

I was living in Japan then, and every evening after dinner I walked into a neighborhood where the houses were cramped and crooked like too many teeth. I would wind my way back and forth until I found, almost by instinct, the dojo where I learned judo. My sensei was one of the most proficient players in the world, but his teaching surpassed his expertise at judo. One night, after a particularly demoralizing experience, I was sitting on the edge of the tatami mat. I had just tried to overpower a much smaller, younger opponent and decidedly lost my match. I was simultaneously angry, embarrassed, and humiliated, and I had no room in my heart for healing. Sensei saw my suffering and chose that moment to teach us a mind-over-matter technique. In order for the technique to work, we had to get free of mental entanglement. In seconds, the anger and frustration drained from my mind and my body became relaxed and alert. The only embarrassment I felt was that the other boys would see the tears of joy welling up and think they were formed out of humiliation. I wiped the tears on the sleeve of my judo-gi while no one was looking.

Immediately, I was struck by the simplicity of this state of inner strength. I didn't have to work or plan or manipulate. On the contrary, I only had to let go of all those things. I didn't understand fully what had happened to me, but I knew that the noisy, conflicted world of adults could not work in the stillness of my heart. It did not have all the answers. Although there were many other similar experiences during my childhood and teens, this single occurrence kept me from completely buying into the precepts of power. On the edge of that tatami mat, I found freedom forgotten. Now, whenever I began to be seduced by the glitz and glitter of the good life, a wee small voice deep inside my breast restlessly stirs and whispers, "Do not go gently into that good night."

The Outward and Inward Paths

I didn't know it at the time, but the inner experience of empty fullness I had in that Yokohama dojo decades ago set me on a path that would alter the way I thought and perceived the world for decades to come. I turned away from the outward materialistic path of power and problems. I traded it for the gentler inward path of peace and... problems. Yes, that's right...the inner path and outer path differ only in direction. They are ultimately paths pot holed with problems that only give the illusion of movement toward the resolution of suffering. A path, by any other name, is still a path, and paths cannot take you to where you already are.

Most of us align ourselves with one of two apparent directions to fulfillment. The first is the most common. It is the outward path toward more and more—the way of self-indulgence. This path satisfies ego by adding more to the menu of life—more money, more education, more friends, more muscles, more beauty, more food, and so on. Here our egos practice gluttony of all kinds, but the driving desire behind it all is never satiated.

The second direction toward fulfillment is the apparent inward path of self-denial—the path of less. Not so commonly traveled as its evil twin, the inward path encourages fasting the ego of outward fare in favor of unadorned "spiritual" practices. Here ego attaches to the idea of sacrifice and other austerities. Removing one's consciousness from outward temptations is an earmark of the inward path.

Both the inward and outward paths are paths nonetheless. Both are telling us that where we are is not good enough and just by beginning our travels we will be rewarded with a better life. But alas, both paths are ineffective in eliminating our most basic desire—the one for lasting peace. There is a concise and poignant text that addresses this problem of attachment to a path or attachment of any kind. Verse 9 of Isa Upanishad, somewhere in the neighborhood of 3,000 years old, tells us:

> *"Those attached to the material world [the outward path]*
> *are damned. Those attached to the spiritual world*
> *[the inward path] are doubly damned."*

I know that most of us think that materialistic overindulgence is more limiting than meditation and scriptural study when it comes to knowing Self, but Isa Upanishad begs to differ. Here's why.

You have probably noticed that it is easier to persuade an alcoholic or a workaholic that their lives are in need of repair than it is someone who is "spiritual." Anyone who leads the outward life already knows deep inside that it doesn't work. They fail to feel forever full no matter how much success they achieve. No matter how many French fries they eat, new cars they own, or people they love, they continually hear their faint inner voice pushing them on, "Not enough. Not yet full."

On the other hand, the spiritual aspirant, no matter what discipline or authority they follow, is convinced that they are on the perfect path to salvation. Even their suffering and "spiritual" failures are interpreted as lessons along the path and encouragement to continue. Suffering and austerities are often worn as badges of courage to be displayed as evidence of their devotion. In fact, failure only strengthens their resolve and encourages more of the same. But the gates of heaven cannot be opened through sheer will only. This is what prompted Jesus to tell us that good deeds alone will not get us into heaven. Isa Upanishad takes it a step further when it warns that the person on the inward path is "doubly damned." It is almost impossible to shake them free from their belief that they will reach complete salvation through dogged determination and spiritual practice.

"Well," you say, "If both the inward and outward paths cannot free us, are we doomed to suffer at the hands of ego's disoriented drive for distinction?"

Of course not. In both cases, the inward and outward paths will bring us to the door of salvation but not how we think. It is not the path that alleviates suffering or brings peace. In fact, the path works by negation. It is when one pauses on the path that they are positioned for success. Success is born of stillness, not movement. Let's see how this is accomplished.

The outward materialistic path works in two instances. When a person fails so miserably to attain their vision of even a minimal existence they will, after great hardship, just give up. This is referred to as "hitting bottom." The other way the materialistic path works is when someone gets everything they need and still they feel empty. They find themselves asking, "Is this all there is to life?" Both complete failure and complete success are valuable in terms of finding inner peace because they shatter the illusion that the path will free them from struggle. All the travelers in between are lost in the illusion that reaching the goal will end their distress. That is called the "rat race." Are you beginning to see the subtle insanity that has worked its way into our thinking? Let's go on.

Instead of focusing on materialistic wealth, the inward path targets Self-awareness. It can also work but only in spite of itself. The transition from ignorance to Self-awareness can take many years. At least that has been the general consensus up until now. QE has a much abbreviated timeline in mind. The inward path to peace is directed toward devotion, meditation, prayer, charitable acts, scriptural inquiry, etc. If you were on the "path to peace," traditionally you would meditate or pray quietly and endeavor to experience a peaceful, blissful state, the result of connection with a higher being or energy. Then your hope would be to carry that inner quiet and guidance, unspoiled, into the shameless outer world. Unfortunately, when inner guidance was lost in the outer world, it was seen as failure and more stringent austerities were prescribed. The veiled thinking was that you could overwhelm the outer world with inner peace if you could only make your peace strong enough.

This approach appears to work only occasionally and over a long period of time. If one becomes Self-aware, it is in spite of the process, not because of it. One reason it takes so long is because the inward path sets the world at war with itself. Peace and divine guidance become the good guys in white and materialism and negative behavior the bad guys in black. Where is the perfection in that? Anytime you have two of anything, you cannot have complete peace. One cannot be unified by dividing and conquering. If you have only one, it must be at peace with itself. There is nothing to oppose its oneness. What more peaceful state could there be than one? Furthermore, there can be only one "one."

Pure awareness is one. When our common awareness becomes aware of pure awareness, it is reflected in the mind as eternal peace. Awareness of pure awareness is nothing more than the realization that common awareness is pure awareness. To become aware of pure awareness and the resultant Self-awareness, all one need do is stop trying...stop doing.

So, in terms of finding everlasting inner peace, neither the outward nor the inward paths are very efficient. There is a reason for that. There is no need for a path. In fact, following any path will ensure that you *will not* arrive at Self-awareness. If you believe you must go somewhere to obtain pure awareness or that you can even acquire it in the first place, you have already lost your way.

Either path—inward or outward—is struggle. Despite our experience to the contrary, we believe that struggle will eventually buy us lasting peace. Peace cannot be found along the path or in reaching the goal. That's right. Reaching a goal does not bring peace. This is perhaps the grandest illusion of all. As soon as we reach one goal, we turn our minds to the next one, isn't that true? The 20th century philosopher Nisargadatta pointed out that anything you can get, you can lose. Lasting peace is no different.

"But wait a minute," you object. "If I don't have lasting peace now, and I can't get it by effort, then why should I even try?"

That's it exactly! You shouldn't try. In fact, you can't try to get perpetual peace because you already have it. It is the trying that creates the waves of distortion on the waters of peace. You see? When you stop...stop...stop....peace is there.

It's not the goal that brings peace but rather the momentary suspension of effort after reaching one goal and before starting another. It is the pause that refreshes, perpetually. It is akin to the gap between your thoughts. In this still silence, one is at peace if only fleetingly so. When one stops, there is nothing to do, nowhere to go. All burden has been lifted. Only then are we free of the illusion that the path will fix our problems. It is ego—not recognizing that the journey has ended and there is no need to continue—who restarts the motor of mind and points it again outward or inward.

So, if the materialistic outward path and the spiritual inward path don't work, are we doomed to flail forever in the waters of discontent? Of course not. Could I let that happen to you? There is a third path that works easily and quickly because it is not really a path at all. QE is unique in its approach to Self-awareness. It is the technique-less technique. QE is successful only when it eliminates itself as a technique and we are left with neither need nor inclination to try.

But here's the neat part. You don't have to give up your path. Whether you are inward- or outward-oriented doesn't matter. Both will work beautifully as long as you add Self-awareness. So, you can put your feet up and watch TV or sequester yourself deep within a cave, and as long as you are Self-aware, either path will yield to inner peace through Self-awareness. This way you really can have your cake and eat it, too. Continue your lifestyle as you love it. There is no need to change. Just become aware of Self and all will work out quickly and for your best benefit. There are many ways to do this, but the QE process is the simplest and most effective way I know. I guess that is obvious or I wouldn't have written a whole book to tell you about it.

I am having fun with you, that's true. But all that I've said is also true. QE actually combines the inward and outward paths simultaneously. What do you have when you go in and out at the same time? You have no movement, right? The "in" and "out" negate themselves and you end up sitting still. What's another word for non-movement? We've already learned that no movement is absolute peace. So, how do we accomplish this technique of non-movement? I'll explain it all in my next book...... Just kidding. All you have to do is turn the page and then get ready to learn this most remarkable technique of not-doing—the Quantum Entrainment process.

CHAPTER 6

Quantum Entrainment

Watch your ever-changing life, probe deeply beyond the motives beyond your actions, and you will soon prick the bubble in which you are enclosed.

Nisargadatta

Doing can never get you to that which you already are. Trace the idea that starts the doing back to its root. There you will find the end of the journey that is never begun.

H.W.L. Poonja

Let me underscore that being Self-aware is not a process but a perception. It is the shift from trying to fix your world to completely accepting it. And keep in mind, this shift happens automatically and without effort. It takes place immediately without trying. When you do Quantum Entrainment (QE), you become aware of pure awareness and then become Self-aware. At that exact moment, you are in harmony with not only your life but every created thing that crawls, flies, or twinkles in the skies. Pretty amazing, huh?

Once Self-aware, no problem will be more than you can handle. You may doubt it in the beginning, but soon you will languish in the protective arms of peace while the fury of life rages on without you. You will begin to identify with silence more and activity less. You will wonder why people are getting so upset, and then you'll realize that those same events upset you not so very long ago. Established in your Self, problems are no more than impish children straining at the bonds of convention. They are not good. They are not bad. They just are. You observe the wondrous workings of the universe as it is right now. It is exactly the same as it has always been and yet very different. Now is forever permeated with the indescribable fullness of peace.

Complete acceptance places you beyond the stroke of the sword of suffering. Beyond the reach of your senses, you sense Perfection. You are Perfection. Discovering your Self, shimmering silently in the heart of every created thing, you come to know God. You come to know your Self as God.

There is more, for there is more than God. God is defined by His/Her/Its creation. God only exists because creation exists. Beyond God is the Nothing from which God arose. And Nothing is absolute peace. You do not need to understand God or Nothing. You do not need to manage the pieces of your life to know Wholeness. You need only this: to do QE and innocently go about your life. That is the single mantra, the sole sermon of peace. It is just that simple.

QE is a process that alters our perception by eliminating movement, leaving us Self-aware. Then in that non-moving state of pure awareness we add back the thoughts and things of our world. It's like turning the movie of your life off and viewing the white screen that supports it. Then turning your life-story back on you will have a different, more expanded, even compassionate perspective of your life. You will begin to appreciate the permanence of Self-awareness under the rocky road you have come to embrace as your life's journey.

Also, without effort, this new perception creates feelings of peace and love and joy. This is the reflection of pure awareness in the mind that we have already discussed. This is the birth of Self and it feels very, very good. These good feelings I call Eufeelings.

Eufeelings

A Eufeeling is unique in all creation. It is the first manifestation of fullness through which the stuff of the cosmos must pass before it becomes a ranch-style house, a butterfly or a flowing river of lava. A Eufeeling is completely safe. It is the only created thing that is free of restriction and contradiction. It is completely open and free flowing.

To the mind, the Eufeeling is rich dark chocolate, a new love, and a rocket ride to heaven all rolled into one. To be cognizant of Eufeeling is the definitive goal of the mind. When it is, the mind yearns for nothing. Established in awareness of Eufeeling, the mind is safe. It can pick its way between the horrors and hardships of life and always feel that mother is watching, waiting with open arms to protect and comfort.

What exactly is a Eufeeling? Good question. Your mind identifies Eufeelings as joy, peace, stillness, silence, unbounded love, bliss, ecstasy, etc. Eufeelings are not to be confused with the everyday garden variety emotions we experience as happiness, excitement, anger, grief, conditional love, jealousy, fear, and so on. These emotions I call conditional feelings because they are born of circumstance like getting money, losing money, losing a loved one, getting a new job, etc.

Conditional feelings are also associated with the past or future. We get anxious or angry or happy when we entertain distant memories or even those made seconds earlier and when we think about what our future holds. The strength of these emotions is also conditional. The strength of a conditional feeling is determined by the mind, both conscious and subconscious. Talk about your can of worms. It all gets pretty convoluted and certainly is not worth our exploring at this juncture. Fortunately, Eufeelings are utterly simple and free of cause and effect.

Actually there is only one Eufeeling which is too subtle to define with a word and yet your mind must label. Change is the nature of the mind. So that single, subtle Eufeeling is experienced by your mind as different flavors or colors. It's like the ocean on different days. One day it is deep blue; another day it is gray/green and so on. That sole Eufeeling reflecting from deep within the mind is recognized as peace or joy or stillness. So, the primal Eufeeling is not really a feeling at all. But it leaves impressions in the mind that are interpreted as quiet, beautiful feelings that uplift the spirit and fill the empty heart.

I'll let you in on a little secret. The Eufeeling is the Self. That's right. Your Self reflects in your mind as joy and love and peace. Remarkable, isn't it? Your Self is beyond the sight of your mind just as the rays of sunlight that color the ocean are beyond the capacity of your eyes to see them. But the first stirring of Self in the mind can be recognized, and that is when you feel peace.

Do you see the implication here? If your Self reflects as Eufeelings, then your Self is all good. Let's not just toss this pearl in the mud. This is a profound discovery and should be explored completely.

If you are thinking of your Self as something "over there" or at the bottom of your mind, then you haven't realized who, or more accurately what, you are. You are still identifying with your body/mind. You are that Eufeeling, nothing less. Remember the Self is unbounded and eternal. And we just found out that it is all good and reflects that goodness in the mind. Only when the mind forgets the Self does the body/mind feel pain and suffering. When you forget your Self, you are like a king with amnesia. Until you regain your memory and reclaim your throne, you will continue to live like a pauper. And lucky for all of us, regaining your memory and reclaiming your throne just happens to be extraordinarily simple.

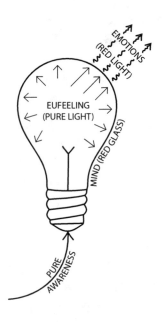

If your mind were a light bulb, then the electricity passing into it would be pure awareness. The clear light that emanated from the filament would be the Eufeeling which would travel outward and strike the glass which represents the outer, individual mind. The unbounded Eufeeling light passing through the mind-glass becomes individualized. Here is where conditional feelings are created. If the glass was blue, then you would radiate depression. Anger might be a red bulb while happiness might be yellow. As the pure Eufeeling passes through the glass of the bulb, it is changed by the individuality of the light bulb. This is where the Eufeeling becomes individualized as anger, melancholy, or happiness.

The point here is that Eufeelings are always pure and clear; always. No matter what you feel or think or do outwardly, inside you is the clear reflection of your Self, of Eufeeling. If someone were to judge you by the color of your reflection, then they would miss the most beautiful expression of you, and themselves—the Eufeeling.

Doing QE enlivens the mind with Eufeelings, and automatically the mind becomes harmonious. From there it reflects harmony into the environment for the benefit of all. Through QE, we spontaneously enjoy the Eufeeling flavor of the moment reflecting in our mind. We also learn to recognize this inner purity of others. We look past the reflected imperfections and see the vibrating peace and stillness of their Eufeeling and we recognize it as our own. It is on the level of Eufeeling awareness that we truly are all one.

How I Discovered QE

We have spent enough time talking about pure awareness, Self-awareness, and Eufeelings. It's time to roll up our sleeves and...do nothing. QE, you will remember, is a process that eliminates movement so that our perception—like a flat shell settling to the bottom of the ocean—moves away from the concerns of the day to settle easily on pure awareness. You will also remember that pure awareness is not all that entertaining to our minds so it gets bored very quickly and returns—like a bubble from the bottom of the sea—to the much more active level of consciousness.

Many very effective healing techniques do just this whether they are aware of it or not. They drop into the perfect harmony of pure awareness and then return to a more active level of mind to administer the healing. The very awareness that heals—pure awareness—is left behind in favor of activating a healing process or modality. The restless mind, unable to find pure awareness of significant interest turns outward toward more entertaining endeavors. What power they would wield if only they could find a way to stay attached to the source of healing. The healing power of their procedure would be incredibly enhanced. Such a procedure would not only be effective at healing physical and emotional concerns but would be the template for healing every facet of one's life: spiritual, social, educational, environmental, political, physical, and mental. Well, hold on to your hats, troopers, because here it comes!

QE is just that process. It is (and I say this in all humility) an astounding stroke of genius. I discovered it not through any superior mental prowess or sharply honed powers of observation. (Anyone who knows me will quickly agree on this point.) Quite the contrary; I discovered the art of non-trying from years of failure at trying. (See Appendix B.) I failed completely at both the inward and outward paths. I completely gave up on both and that is when it struck me that the hidden third path had been in plain sight all the time.

When I surrendered to what was and stopped trying to fix anything, the heavens parted and a celestial sun shone down so brightly I had to get sunglasses for my third eye. I felt marvelous! And when I examined that marvelous feeling more closely, it grew in intensity. There was no reason for my elation other than stopping what I was doing and observing to see what happened. I didn't try and find a reason for what was happening. My mind was thrilled to be right where it was. As soon as I did try to analyze what was happening, I lost my sense of joy and unbounded presence. So, I stopped trying and again my Eufeeling came flooding back. It was all so simple and so powerful. In the words of Padahasta, it was as plain as the fruit in the palm of my hand.

In a very short time, I did learn to hold this state of Eufeeling while I went about my daily activities. Slowly at first and then more vigorously, I was able to be aware of pure awareness and the Eufeeling during the most dynamic of activities. Now few activities overshadow my perception of Eufeeling, and when it is lost, it is only for a few moments. Then it instinctively returns and we embrace like the dear, old friends we are.

How to Do QE

I hope you are ready to learn QE because I'm ready to teach you. I've been excited about this moment since I started writing this book and I think I've been patient enough. Are you ready? Then let's get started.

In preparation, find yourself a quiet place with a comfortable chair where you won't be disturbed by family, friends, pets, or phones for a full 30 minutes. You can also have somebody read these instructions to you as long as they only read what is written and do not engage you in conversation. Or you can record the instructions, making sure to leave blank space when instructions call for time with eyes closed. OK, ready?

Sit comfortably and close your eyes. Just let your mind wander wherever it wants to go for 15–30 seconds. Just watch your thoughts as they come and go. Now, become more aware of what you are thinking. The content doesn't matter. Just pay very close attention to any thoughts that flow across the screen of your mind. Watch them with focused attention. That doesn't mean you should make an effort to try and watch them or concentrate on them. Be easy with a focused attention like a cat watching a mouse hole. Continue to watch your thoughts with an easy, focused attention for one to two minutes.

Don't read any further until you have closely watched your thoughts for one or two minutes. I'll wait...

OK, have you just finished one or two minutes, attentively watching your thoughts? Good, then let's continue.

As you observed your thoughts, you will have noticed that they became quieter and slowed down almost immediately, isn't that right? They didn't seem as loud. They became fainter and fewer in between as your thinking became softer. Remember that whatever your thoughts are doing is just right. Whether your thoughts are noisy or quiet doesn't matter; your job is to be the perfect observer. You just watch to see what they'll do next. That's all you must do; observe with quiet attention.

Did you happen to notice that at times your thoughts stopped all together? As your thoughts became fainter, you may have noticed that they died away and you were left alone with just pure awareness. Neat, huh? But we're just getting started.

Do you also notice that after you did the first part of this exercise that you felt more relaxed in the body and more quiet in the mind?

These are delicious benefits of becoming aware of pure awareness, whether you were aware of it or not. Soon you will be functioning on this quiet, more refined level even while you are in rush hour traffic. But we have more to do so let's get back to it.

Again, close your eyes. Innocently and with attention watch your thoughts as before. This time it will be easier and you might find your thoughts quickly settling down or stopping altogether. Attentively observe in this way for a couple of minutes. After two or three minutes note how you feel.

Again, I'll wait...

During those two or three minutes, did you feel some stillness, silence, or peace? You may also have felt joy, love, compassion, elation, bliss, etc. The good feeling that you experienced is your Eufeeling.

This time when you sit with your eyes closed, this is what I would like you to do. Watch your thoughts and wait for your Eufeeling to rise in your awareness. Remember, your Eufeeling could be something as simple as stillness or silence or as profound as ecstasy. One Eufeeling in no better than another. Whatever your Eufeeling is, just easily observe it. If thoughts return, innocently observe them. Then your thoughts will give way to either no-thought, pure awareness or your Eufeeling. Whichever is there—thoughts, Eufeeling, or pure awareness—observe it with simple innocence and do nothing else. This is very important; do nothing but watch your thoughts and wait for your Eufeeling. When your Eufeeling is in your awareness, focus on it clearly and intently. At times you may have neither Eufeeling nor thoughts. That is pure awareness. At that time you simply wait in pure awareness until your

Eufeeling rises again.

Do you see how simple this is? Whatever appears on the screen of your mind, your position is always the same. You are the observer, nothing more. *Never interfere or try to control either your thoughts or your Eufeeling.* Believe me; everything will be taken care of for you. Did you have to work at becoming relaxed or feeling peaceful? No, it's all automatic. It's all taken care of for you through the wisdom of your Eufeeling once you become aware of it. Don't complicate it or you will step back on the path to struggle and suffering.

Now resume the QE process with eyes closed just as I have described it above. Do this session for about five minutes. When you are done, take enough time to slowly open your eyes and continue reading.

How are you feeling right now? Are you aware of your Eufeeling right now? Guess what? Your eyes are open and you are aware of your Eufeeling. Isn't that remarkable? Before you had to close your eyes and dive deep within your mind to find it. But look what has happened. Your Eufeeling has followed you out into activity. How cool is that?

Remember that your Eufeeling is unbounded so it is always there. You have just been ignoring it most of your life. And you will ignore it again, but very quickly by doing QE regularly, you will always have it in a moment's reflection. You are building the foundation for a life that is beyond imagination. Somewhere in the not-too-distant future, you will all of a sudden realize that you are living life in bliss, beyond your greatest expectations.

Now, we are not quite done. In fact, the best is just ahead. I'd like you to continue with the QE process as you have just learned it. Close your eyes and observe what is flowing across the screen of your mind. Watch until you become aware of your Eufeeling and then observe it with tender attention. Not interfering, look deeply into Eufeeling. If it changes into another Eufeeling, then look deeply into the new one. Do this for 3–5 minutes.

Then when you feel the time is right, slowly open your eyes and continue doing QE. Sitting with eyes open staring easily ahead of you, become aware of your Eufeeling. Continue to do QE with eyes open.

You will have thoughts, Eufeeling, and pure awareness all with your eyes open. Continue for one or two minutes more and then slowly stand and look at some object nearby. Look at the object and then become aware of your Eufeeling. Then look at another object while observing your Eufeeling.

When you are ready, slowly walk around the room. Feel your body moving. Feel how you balance on one leg, then the other and the pressure of the floor against each foot. When your Eufeeling is not there, just find it again through simple awareness. As you walk slowly around the room, engage all your senses. Pay attention to the noises in the room. Feel the air brush past your face. Run your hand over a plant or another object. Engage your sense of smell and taste. All the while, continue to return to your Eufeeling when you notice it is not there. Stop and become solely aware of your Eufeeling and feel how it intensifies or changes into a different Eufeeling. In actuality, it doesn't really change in intensity or kind. You are just becoming more aware of the infinite manifestations of your Self. This is You the way you were meant to be. Not all tangled up in the ego-manipulated activities founded on fear but just simply being with your Self. Nothing is more important or fulfilling.

QE REVIEW

- Sit comfortably with your eyes closed and let your thoughts wander for 10–15 seconds

- Watch your thoughts with simple innocence like a cat watching a mouse hole

- In time, your thoughts will become quieter or slower or disappear altogether

- Continue to quietly observe whatever happens

- Soon you will feel a good feeling, your Eufeeling

- Now observe your Eufeeling with clear but simple innocence

- It will get stronger or change into another Eufeeling or thoughts will come

- Whatever happens, just observe it unfolding as if you were watching a movie

- When you open your eyes, continue this simple process of innocent observation

- Move around the room, slowly interacting with objects

- When you realize your Eufeeling has slipped away, just look to see what you are feeling. Observe it for awhile, then continue to explore other object

CHAPTER 7

Applying QE

*Whenever an answer, a solution, or a creative idea
is needed, stop thinking for a moment by focusing
attention on your inner energy field.*

Eckhart Tolle

*If you inhibit thought (and persevere), you come at
length to a region of consciousness below or behind thought...
and a realization of an altogether vaster self than that
to which we are accustomed.*

Edward Carpentier

Basic QE

The process you learned above is basic Quantum Entrainment (QE). It is the foundation for all QE applications. This is all you need to be Self-aware. But if you want to apply QE in other areas of your life—like improving relationships and eliminating physical pain—then you will need to learn how to apply this basic process to common everyday situations, especially if you what to help others enjoy the power of your newfound awareness. I will explain the more specific applications of QE in the appropriate chapters, but you will want to literally reach out and help others. Doing QE for others is exciting and a lot of fun, so I will offer you a few general rules to follow that will open your awareness to the world.

Authors note: *If you want to focus specifically on healing with QE, then I suggest you read* The Secret of Instant Healing *by this author. It will afford the reader a deeper understanding of the specific healing applications of QE.*

Physical QE

When you want to share QE with others, you can do so physically or remotely. Physical QE means that you physically touch your partner and Remote QE means that you don't touch them. That's pretty simple. Let's take a look at how you do Physical QE.

Approach your partner quietly and let them know that you are going to touch them lightly. You can let them know that the whole process will only last from a few seconds to a few minutes. By way of explanation, you can tell them:

Rest is the universal healer. Everything needs rest to heal. The deeper the rest, the deeper the healing that takes place. I have learned the QE process that will allow your body a very deep rest in a very short time and permit deep healing to take place.

Now place your hand on your partner's body. Your touch should be as light as a finger on an eyeball. When you touch them, don't rub or massage or move your hand in any way. It is important to know that it doesn't matter where you put your hands. Healing will occur even if you don't touch them. Some people like the hands-on approach and others prefer remote. Maybe because of my Chiropractic background, I prefer to touch when I can. Some of my favorite places are the neck, forehead, lower back, and upper chest. I go to these places out of habit, not because they help the healing in any way. Pure awareness doesn't need my help.

Just make contact with both hands and ask them not to try and help in any way. Tell them, "Just let your mind wander wherever it wants to go."

Once your hands are firmly but gently on your partner's body, do the QE process. And then...well, that's it. You don't do anything else but QE.

Maintain awareness of your Eufeeling or pure awareness or whatever is in your mind just like you learned. Remember you are not healing them or creating energy that will heal them. You are doing nothing but QE. It's so cool. While their body/mind is going through a metamorphosis of major proportions, you are just hanging out in bliss. Does it get any better than that?

You can move your hands occasionally but not too often as that may be a little unsettling for your partner. I suggest you move one hand and then the other, but not both at the same time. When you are done with the session, just step away.

During the session, your partner may begin to sway like a tree in a soft breeze. Make sure he doesn't tip over. QE is very relaxing, and his body may want to move in some strange positions as he releases the physical knots locked in the muscle fibers. Just be there to support him and keep him from falling.

I went to visit some friends at an alternative healing fair. They had a Kirlian camera that took pictures of the colors around people that represent emotions. A woman had just gotten her picture taken and she showed me the bubbles and balloons of many colors around her head and shoulders. She asked me what I did and I told her QE. When people hear this, the most common response I get is a quick frown followed by a vapid smile and an utterance of, "Oh, that's nice." This woman was no different, so I offered to show her what I did. As soon as I touched her, she fell straight backwards. Had I not been prepared, she would have fallen hard on the floor. I eased her down and then helped her up a couple of minutes later. She said she felt fine and my friends with the Kirlian camera suggested she take another picture. This time she had only one color: a solid gold rainbow from shoulder to shoulder. I'm not up on my Kirlien colors, but she and my friends seemed to think the change was pretty nifty. The point, in a round-about way is that if I hadn't been ready to catch her, she could have been hurt in the fall. Now, this is an extreme case as 99% of the people who receive QE enjoy a soft, gentle rocking as their muscles and emotions drain of stress.

Remote QE

Remote QE is pretty much like Physical QE except you don't touch your partner. If you are in the same room, this is not much of a concern. But if your partner is in the next county visiting Aunt Tilley and her three-legged dog on the ostrich farm, then Remote QE is just what the doctor ordered. Here's how to do Remote QE.

When you do QE remotely, have your partner sit quietly, with her eyes closed and remind her to let her mind wander where it will. Let her know how long you are going to do QE and then have her call or e-mail you after the session. Let her call you because she may want to stay in that blissful state for some time after or she may fall asleep and let deeper healing take over. It's also a good idea to do a pre- and post-test on the problem, whether it is physical or emotional. You'll learn how to do that in the next section of this book.

I do Remote QE sessions with people all over the world. Sometimes I don't know anything about that person, including what they want to heal or even what their name is. QE still works. That is because pure awareness is not ignorant or directionally challenged. It knows what to do because it created the apparent problem and knows where to go because it is already there. I am only a witness to what is taking place despite the urgings of my ego to the contrary.

Remote QE is great fun and just as beneficial for the QE-er as it is the QE-ee. My wife Martina, a massage therapist for professional athletes, works very hard to keep her clientele happy. After a strenuous massage session with a many-muscled athlete, she will walk sweating into my office and see me working remotely with a client. I am sitting quietly in a comfortable overstuffed chair deep in bliss. As she passes by, I can hear her humph me under her breath as if to say, "Get a real job."

If you have a good imagination, you can imagine your partner is with you in the room or you are there with her or you both meet in an imaginary Starbuck's for QE and coffee. Anyway, in your imagination you simply do what you would do if the partner were with you physically. See yourself starting just as you would in person and then do QE. What you do is not important. That you do QE, however, is vitally important.

You can also use a surrogate like a doll to stand in for the absent partner. Place your hands on the doll as if it were your partner. You can also use your own body as a surrogate. The easiest way to do this is sitting and then contacting your thighs or somewhere easy to reach and then do QE. You can also use pictures or even write the partner's name on a piece of paper. Your surrogate can also be another human. Just work on a friend as if they were the partner and all three of you will heal. Finally, you can do what I call "air QE" much like the air guitar players who forgot their guitars at home. All these props are unnecessary except as an aid for your mind. So don't be fooled into thinking that you need a picture of the person or must know what problems he is working on. Just remember that pure awareness will manifest the proper healing at the proper time and the proper place. You just get to watch.

Extended QE

Extended QE is also pretty much what it sounds like. Instead of QE-ing for a minute or two, you do it for extended periods up to an hour. Most often Extended QE is combined with Remote QE. I usually do 20 minute sessions.

Extended QE offers the partner—not to mention the initiator—a chance for longer exposure to pure awareness, opening his body/mind to more profound healing. Extended periods are most beneficial for deep emotional trauma and chronic physical conditions.

Start Extended QE as you would a basic session. As more time unfolds and you remain anchored in pure awareness, you may find your mind floating up to dwell on the levels of subtler energy and you may see the patterns of creative healing forces swirling and flowing around you. Here you may receive great insights as to how the universe works or find solutions to problems on the grosser level of everyday life. You may also be visited by angels or disincarnate masters and other distractions. Resist the urge to wander off from pure awareness and play at this time. Your job is to do QE, remaining aware of your Eufeeling and pure awareness. Everything else is just window dressing. You will gain more than you can ever imagine by lingering on the finest level of the mind free of entanglement. You can play with the angels later, I promise.

With all forms of QE healing, the effects will continue to manifest long after the session. Even if nothing seemed to happen right away, 20 minutes or 20 days later the healing may be complete. I often post-test right after the session. Then after I talk to the partner for a minute or two, I test again and there is significant improvement. I once had a woman in one of my seminars who had tinnitus for 30 years. I did QE for about a minute and she had no change. Before lunch I asked her to check her condition again and still no change. The same was true at the end of the day. Three days later, however, she called me and said that when she woke up, her tinnitus was 80% improved and she was ecstatic. So, just a reminder not to get too attached to results. Pure awareness always works but almost never how we think it will.

REVIEW OF SECTION I

- The primary question that every one of us should entertain is, "How can I be free of the need to control?"

- The problem is that we don't need more. We need less. In fact, we need less than less. We need nothing.

- When you add the idea if Nothing, along with the experience of Nothing, it has a most remarkable effect on us. It removes suffering.

- The ego is always looking to add something to enhance its existence. Ego creates suffering.

- QE process works by subtraction. It offers your mind less and less until Nothing is left.

- You are the pure awareness of Nothing, the gap between thoughts.

- Pure awareness is everywhere, all the time.

- Thoughts appear spontaneously from pure awareness beyond the control of our mind.

- Peace dawns with the realization that we are not in control.

- When we live life free of the desire to control, we not only gain inner peace but prosper outwardly as well.

- Our Self is unique in all creation. It has a foot on both worlds; the absolute sea of pure awareness and the multi-splintered expressions of the created cosmos. It is totally harmless and completely nurturing.

- It is impossible for our minds to understand either pure awareness or our Self.

- Paths only give the illusion of movement toward the resolution of suffering.

- Reaching a goal cannot bring lasting peace.

- QE actually creates no movement with the realization of pure awareness.

- Eufeeling is Self.

- Eufeeling reflects in the mind as joy, peace, stillness, silence, unbounded love, bliss, ecstasy, etc.

- QE is Self-awareness, anchoring the mind in the joy of Eufeeling.

- Self-awareness, QE, enriches life on every level.

- Anyone can do QE. QE is the birthright of every human.

SECTION II
Quantum Living

Arrows of hate have been shot at me, too, but they never hit me,
because somehow they belonged to another world with which I
have no connection whatsoever. I live in that solitude which is
painful in youth, but delicious in the years of maturity.

Albert Einstein

Two birds, inseparable companions, perch on the same tree.
One eats the fruit, the other looks on. The first bird is our
individual self, feeding on the pleasures and pains of this
world. The other is the universal Self, silently witnessing all.

Mundaka Upanishad

Overview

Learning Quantum Entrainment (QE) is a revelation for most people. They realize that despite what their parents, teachers, friends, and civic, spiritual, and political leaders have been telling them, they do not have to work hard for a lifetime to find the peace and contentment they crave. On the contrary, following the conventional outward or inward paths will most often find a soul clamoring for the innocence of childhood. When QE is experienced for the first time, most people stand in awe at the simplicity and speed at which deep relaxation and inner peace materialized within them and the outer healing it brings with it. It is at this moment that they realize it has always been within them, waiting patiently for recognition. What an absolute joy to finally realize that the kingdom of heaven is within you and you don't have to do anything to get it.

In this section, you will learn how to enjoy your newfound inner awareness while performing the mundane and not so mundane tasks of everyday living. You will learn how to be aware of pure awareness while traveling, eating, walking, making love, sleeping, and much more. You will learn to heal emotional upset in yourself and others and administer the soothing salve of pure awareness to reduce and eliminate physical pain and problems.

In the beginning, as you practice QE you will start to develop a sense of being at home. That is, you will feel that nature, people, and even inanimate objects share with you the common bond of awareness. Everywhere you will find friendliness reflecting back to you. Your ego will expand beyond its individual need for power and you will relax into the long rejected role of being fully human.

As you continue your practice of QE, your senses will refine and things will take on a softer feel, a kind of porous shimmering as if everything were alive. And it is alive with awareness. As your senses refine, you will discover joy in the most unsuspecting places: a dead leaf struggling to free itself from the branch and return to the earth, the lopsided gait of a homeless man as he steps up on the curb, or heat waves rising from the hood of your car in rush hour traffic. There is nowhere that pure awareness is not. The more places you discover it, the more you will be surprised to find your Self smiling back at you.

The following chapters in Section II are arranged into four parts: Mind, Body, Relationships, and Everything Else. These are loose groupings and some overlap will be apparent. I suggest you first read Chapter 8, Healing Negative Emotions. This chapter sets the tone and offers extra information that the others will draw from. Then feel free to read in any order of interest to you. I recommend that you read each chapter completely and then practice the QE exercise. Reread the chapter after a few days of applying QE. This will help remove any effort or alterations you may have inadvertently let creep into your practice. Remember QE's power comes from its simplicity. The more you add to it, or think about it, the less effective it becomes. Less is better; Nothing is best. Effort or trying is opposed to QE. So the cardinal rule is, "If it isn't easy and you're not having fun, then you aren't doing QE."

Are you ready to go? Ready for me to stop gesticulating, pontificating, and generally being a bother? Well, then, what are you waiting for? Turn the page and open an inspiring, exciting new chapter in your life.

Part I: The Mind

CHAPTER 8

Healing Negative Emotions

Great, you've lost all hope.
Frank Kinslow, *Beyond Happiness*

The harder the mind struggles to get rid of pain,
the greater is the pain.

Eckhart Tolle

Reflexively, my head turned toward the sound of a breaking plate, and then more slowly back to the middle-aged woman sitting across from me. We were at a small marbled table in a trendy café. It was an island of equanimity cluttered with mid-morning deserters from a chaotic world that waited, like an expectant father, just beyond the glass doors.

She was a friend, visiting Sarasota for a few weeks to soak up a compassionate winter sun. We had been catching up on each other's lives. She told me about her children, her job, and the health issues she had been battling. She set her cup down and when she raised her eyes, they had lost the sparkle that had played there just moments before. I waited. When she broke the silence, her voice was muted and her mood pensive.

She said with real concern, "You have said that in order to have inner peace, we must lose our hope. Hope is all I have with my diabetes. If I were to lose hope, I would have nothing."

83

"What is wrong with nothing?" I asked.

She looked at me in disbelief. "If I have nothing, I...I lose who I am. Just thinking about it makes me feel empty, abandoned."

She seemed to shrink before my eyes, a kind of caving in on her self.

"Giving up hope," she shared, "Is giving up life!"

"Let's try a little experiment, OK?" I encouraged her. "But you will have to trust me and do exactly as I ask."

She was apprehensive, but she agreed. I asked her to close her eyes. She placed both hands on the table, laced her fingers, and let her flickering eyelids close. Behind her lids, her eyes darted about, not willing to be seduced by the soothing darkness that now surrounded them.

I said, "Let go of your hope. Let nothing take its place. What do you feel?"

After a few uneasy seconds, she protested, "I feel afraid...anxious... I am very uncomfortable. I don't like doing this."

"Stay with me," I encouraged. "Which emotion is the strongest?"

"Fear," she said quietly.

Gently, I instructed, "Instead of turning away from your fear, look at it closely. Become acutely aware of your fear. As you watch it, it will change."

"What is happening to your fear now that you are watching it?" I asked.

"At first it got stronger. I wanted to open my eyes," she replied, "Now it is like a pale shadow. It is like my awareness is the sun and the fear is burning away like fog!"

"Go on. Continue observing your fear," I encouraged.

A few moments later, I noticed a change in her breathing and I asked, "What do you see now?"

"Nothing," she answered.

"Do you feel fear?" I asked.

"No, I feel nothing," she repeated.

I said, "Pay attention to the nothing like you did the fear. What do you feel?"

"I feel completely at peace," she said with some surprise.

Her body was relaxed and her face glowed. Her eyelids had stopped flickering and her eyes were at rest. They must have found what they were looking for.

I asked her to open her eyes and when she did, her lips parted in a huge, spontaneous smile. She asked, "What just happened?"

Fear is a shadow that creates other shadows like anxiety, dread, and remorse. Shadows grow darker in the subconscious when the conscious mind turns away from them. Hope turns the mind away from the present, where peace resides, and entices it to dwell on the future. Hope, like the future, is an illusion. Hope, like happiness, is conditional. Peace is unconditional and always present. Unconditional means it is free from things and ideas and emotions; free from the agony of opposites like right and wrong, birth and death. Nothing is also unconditional and free from opposites. Nothing is the progenitor of peace. We don't really fear nothing. We fear the *idea* of nothing. Peace is the movie screen upon which these shadows are thrown to create the illusion of life. Upon quiet inspection you will see through the phantom of fear, and its specter offspring, to the peace that is radiating just beyond. Peace is always there in the background, like a loving mother watching her child at play.

We spoke of many things that morning and the time to part came quickly. We stood up from the table and looked around the still crowded café.

I said, "You still have diabetes, but without hope, you will be at peace with it."

My friend gave me a big smile and a bigger hug. Then we turned and stepped through the glass doors to embrace the chaos beyond.

Even in a crowded restaurant, a complete novice can become aware of pure awareness. Why? Because is it the most natural state of being for a human being. Does that tell you anything about the way most of us are living our lives? We have lost our way, but pure awareness is a homing beacon radiating peace from every created thing.

In the conversation in the coffee shop, the beacon was fear. Fear is peace. You read that right. Peace resides within all emotions—negative or positive. What we normally do is turn away from negativity and look for relief in positivity. That is the nature of life. However when we turn away from a negative emotion like fear, anger, grief, anxiety, or guilt we actually increase the intensity and longevity of that emotion. I know it sounds counter-intuitive, but if we want to release a destructive emotion, then we must not ignore it or run from it. Conversely, we don't want to declare war on it either. That will only entrench that emotion, ensuring it a safe haven for years to come.

So, what can we do? How can we neutralize the power negative emotions hold over us? In one simple stroke of genius we can deflate the negative influence of emotions like letting air out of a balloon. We neither turn away from, nor wage war on, them. We take the neutral stance of observation but with one very important addition. We observe from the safety of the Self. Wrapped in a blanket of bliss, our psyches are safe from emotional trauma. No negativity can penetrate the mind that is settled fully in the Self. It is impossible. Do you doubt it? Well, then, let's put it to the test.

Sit comfortably in a chair and close your eyes. If you have great emotional trauma in your life, it might do to pick a lesser problem to work on this first time. You'll get to the big ones soon enough and love doing it.

OK, bring up a negative situation, memory, or emotion in your mind. It could be something recent or from childhood, it doesn't really matter. Pay attention to the emotion(s) attached to the situation. Let them get as strong as they can in your mind and when they are as strong as possible, grade them on a scale from 1–10, 10 being absolutely unbearable. Once you've got a number that represents how strong the emotion is, then let the memory go.

Now do Quantum Entrainment (QE). Watch your thoughts with simple innocence just as you learned to do in the first section of this book. Remember that emotions are thoughts. Watch your thoughts/ emotions as they become quieter and begin to fade in intensity. Observe as they disappear altogether, giving rise to your Eufeeling. Consciously identify your Eufeeling and watch it as it changes back into thoughts or other Eufeelings or disappears. Do this for a minute or two or three. You will know when to stop. Then bring up the offending emotional event or memory again—the same as before—and grade 1–10. You will find the negative influence of the memory has significantly reduced in potency or has completely disappeared! The most common response is, "I can't even bring up the emotion attached to this memory."

Negative emotions are shadows that get stronger in your mind when you fight them or turn away from them. QE is like having a light attached to a rheostat. As you turn up the light in a dark room, the shadows lighten and disappear. As the light of pure awareness grows in the mind, harmful emotions dissipate like the harmless specters they are. A QE mind becomes light and lively and full of mirth.

Angry Outbursts

Of course we just neutralized harmful emotions isolated in a safe environment. But what happens when emotions like anger take hold and carry us beyond control? QE'ers are human. In fact, they are more human than before they became reunited with their Self. Being human means experiencing the full range of emotions while Self-aware.

"But," you object, "Isn't that a conflict? How can you be Self-aware and angry or sad at the same time?"

Hey, good question. Remember our discussion about the slow-walking, slow-talking saint being only one flavor of sainthood? Saints come in all kinds of packages just like the non-Self realizers. (I don't think that's a word, but you know what I mean.) Start looking at yourself as a saint at least when you are Self-aware. When Self-aware, you are saintly so don't try to talk yourself out of it.

When you are fully Self-aware, you will notice that you still have emotions—likes and dislikes, preferences and desires—but they are blips on the radar screen; ripples on the ocean of pure awareness. The question is what to do when you have momentarily forgotten your Self and you become overshadowed by an emotion like sadness or anger.

If anger overtakes you, what can you do? Nothing. If it has you in its fiery grip, you won't be able to do a thing until that grip loosens a bit. You can make things worse by trying to stop anger or feeling guilty about it but then you can't stop those feelings when they are in full bloom either.

When you are overtaken by emotion of any kind, don't fight it— just observe. The wheels of anger, anxiety, and remorse turn forcefully, but pure observation will slow those wheels faster than anything else you can do. It's like being caught in a thunderstorm. Just stay where you are looking, waiting for a break in the clouds. Then when the emotional storm clouds begin to clear, you can once again do QE and the emotional clouds will dissipate like mist in the mid-day sun.

Doing QE regularly will tremendously reduce the intensity and frequency of emotional trauma. In time, like the Dalai Lama, you, too, will find the angry waves of an emotional storm have become but ripples on a quiet pond.

Helping Others

You will be amazed at yourself when you apply QE for others who are feeling emotional discord. QE takes the emotion out of the trauma, leaving only an impotent impulse to mark where suffering once thrived. Here's how you employ QE to help others with emotional upset.

Just as you did for yourself, have your partner close her eyes, making the emotion as strong as she can and grade the upset 1–10. Stand or sit during the process—whichever you prefer. Then place your hands on your partner. It doesn't matter where you place your hands or if you use your fingertips, palms, back of your hands, etc. I like to use palms and fingers. I also like to place my hands on my partner's neck, lower back, forehead, and upper chest. There is no reason for this other than it is a habit of mine and it has absolutely no bearing on how effective the healing will be. Practice Emotional QE in a way that is comfortable for both you and your partner. Do this for 2–5 minutes and then have your partner retest. If you are working with your partner remotely, then instruct her to retest after she emerges from the session.

Emotional QE is especially effective when using Extended QE. Increase the time of the QE session and make sure you give your partner more time to transition from the deep quiet of QE to the active world she will reenter.

A Word About Intention

There has been a lot of interest of late about the intention especially around energy healing techniques. Some stress that the intention is of ultimate importance and should therefore be very precise. Some say intentions must be stated free of fear or full of love. There can be many rules and restrictions around intentions. There comes a time when there are so many rules governing how your intention should be framed that one begins to feel a kind of anxiety about proper use. It also appears that the more the healing technique relies on control, the more precise the intention should be. For instance, if you want a new house, then you may be asked to imagine the house you want in every minute detail down to the color of the light switches and the squeak in the garden gate.

I am often asked by those who have done techniques that employ intention how the QE intention should be structured. The answer is simple: the intention is implied. That means that either you or your partner will supply the intention simply by knowing what needs to be fixed. When the partner comes to us and says, "I have a pain in my knee," it's pretty evident to both of you that you want the pain to go away. That is the intention—simple, short, and unobtrusive. It can be nothing more than a fleeting thought such as, "Pain gone."

Since QE is not an energy healing technique, we do not need to be too awfully concerned with intention. In fact, we don't even have to know what problem is bothering our partner. This is especially evident when we work emotionally with QE.

QE is not an energy technique, but it produces energy; otherwise, no healing or improvement in our finances or relationships would take place. The point is that the QE practitioner does not work on the energy level. She does not work at all once the QE process is started.

When you want to plan a trip through an unknown city, you must be very precise. You must plan the trip yourself, making sure you have enough gas and that the car is road ready. When you begin your trip, you have to watch out for the time, weather, traffic, street signs, and land-marks all while driving in unfamiliar surroundings. Or you could hire a cab to drive you while you sit back and enjoy the ride. Pure awareness is our cab. It knows where we want to go and how best to get us there.

CHAPTER 9

Creativity and Overcoming Creative Blocks

*A great many people will think they are thinking when they
are merely rearranging their prejudices.*

William James

*We no more know our own destiny than a tea leaf knows
the destiny of the East India Company.*

Douglas Adams

Does anybody have any idea where ideas come from? How about a
hint? Ideas are thoughts, right? And thoughts come from...pure
awareness. So that means ideas come from pure awareness. Ideas are a
form of creativity and so they must necessarily come from the source of
all creation. It stands to reason that if we want to become more creative,
then it would be good to get close to pure awareness.

Odd as it sounds initially, less action (rest) is the springboard for
action. We see this principle being played out all around us but we
usually just focus on the action part. For instance, we sleep and then
perform activity. Our hearts beat after the rest phase, our eyes blink
and open, and there is a pause between every in and out breath. The
earth rests in winter, and I wonder if the expanding universe will some
day reverse itself and contract back into complete and utter awareness.

Another principle of rest and activity is apparent: The deeper the rest the more dynamic the activity. The most obvious example is sleep. When sleep is shallow and restless, we do not perform our best the following day. We can also interpret this principle in terms of direction by saying that when we want to exert an influence in one direction, we must start by going in the opposite direction. We normally don't look at life this way, but simple inspection will show it to be apparent.

If, for instance, you want to get up from that chair you are sitting in, what is the first action you perform? You push down with your hands and feet in order to stand up, right? If you want to build a skyscraper, then you start by digging a hole. If you want to drive a nail, you start by drawing the hammer in the opposite direction. If you want to shoot an arrow toward a target, you must first pull it in the opposite direction.

If you want to build a bigger skyscraper, drive a nail deeper, or shoot an arrow further, then you must dig a deeper hole, raise the hammer higher, and draw the arrow further back. You can imagine what would happen to a 20-story building if the foundation were only 10 feet deep.

Pure awareness is the deepest rest you can get. Awareness of pure awareness will afford the most dynamic activity. Pure awareness is also found in the opposite direction of any activity. Remember that pure awareness in non-activity so it is always less than any activity you perform. The deepest rest and the most dynamic activity come from being aware of pure awareness.

All of this is pretty obvious and intuitive but we seem to completely miss this principle when it comes to creativity. Our minds most usually chug along in a very active manner. We fire off one thought after another, day after day, year after year, until the body/mind finally dissolves back into the ocean of awareness from which it was born. All during our lives, we pay little attention and less homage to pure awareness and its role in creativity and yet there is no creation or creativity without it.

We become more creative the same way we shoot an arrow. When we shoot an arrow, we draw it back, back, back until it is fully drawn and at rest. At this point the arrow is non-moving but full of potential. Now, what does the archer have to do to get the arrow to the target? All he has to do is aim and relax. Once the arrow is fully drawn, at rest, and properly aimed, all the forces of physics rally to support its unerring flight to the heart of the target.

Creative ideas issue forth from the consciousness of a mind fully drawn and at rest in pure awareness. The consciousness of a chaotic mind is slightly drawn and resultant thought and activity is weak. We don't have to look too far to see how common our senseless, irrational, hurtful deeds have become. Acting from a chaotic mind is like pulling an arrow back only a few centimeters and letting it go. The arrow falls pathetically at the feet of the ineffective archer.

My friend Don and I once took an archery class in college. He had a good deal of trouble with all the fine motor skills that archery presents. The instructor, who was the basketball coach in the fall, had little patience with people who did not show at least a modicum of athletic ability. He continually pointed out Don's shortcomings to the rest of the class, sometimes bellowing and waving his arms as if it were mid-season on the basketball court.

One day the instructor was particularly disturbed and pushed us all to perform with perfect precision. Most of us hit the ground around the target and a few lucky souls actually stuck an arrow in the target. Don was particularly determined this day to make the instructor proud of him by putting one of his arrows dead center in the bull's eye. He took a long, deep draw, holding his breath, arms wobbling like the legs of a newborn calf. The rest of us stood wearily away from the action as Don took aim and released his arrow. Unfortunately, the arrow fell impotently at his feet while the bow leaped forward out of his hand, bounced forward, spun around, and came to rest a full ten feet in front of him. The instructor, face red and eyes bulging, threw up his hands and stomped off the archery court. We all thanked the hapless archer for deflecting the wrath of the instructor and getting us out of class early that day.

I'd like to have some salient or profound point to this story but I don't. I was just writing about archery when this memory popped into my head and I thought I'd share it with you. Now, let's leave Don and his bow and arrow on the archery field and get back the business of being creative.

All this talk about ideas and weak thought and going in the opposite direction to find fulfillment is all well and good, but does it have any practical value? Yes! We can become more creative, or actually allow creativity to flow through us more effortlessly, when we are aware of pure awareness. Thankfully, we already know how to do that. A little tweaking won't hurt, however. Let's take a closer look at how to inspire more creativity in our lives.

How to Plant the Seed of Creativity

This is a pretty short procedure so don't blink your eyes. But you can sit comfortably with your eyes closed. Review all the pertinent points involved in the situation before you do Quantum Entrainment (QE). For instance, if you have writer's block, can't find the right color for your canvas, or are lacking the musical notes for your stalled opus, let your mind run over what you are interpreting as failure. See clearly where you are stuck and then let it go.

Now sit down and do QE. Watch your thoughts as they refine and finally disappear to be replaced with your Eufeeling. Continue to observe your Eufeeling and it will become fuller. Now, while you are completely wrapped in your Eufeeling, have a thought of what you want to create. Just produce one single, simple intention, image, or idea and then step back to watch what happens. For instance, "opus complete" or "canvas full of color." Once is enough! Don't muddy the clear waters of pure awareness. A single, subtle intention while fully aware of Self is absolutely all that is needed. Now, watch and wait.

One of two things will happen. Either the solution will present itself immediately and you are done or nothing will appear to happen. If you don't receive an answer right away then stay in that fullness a little longer if you like. Contrary to those who believe that creativity is born of suffering, creativity blossoms in the fullness of Self. If you decide you must cut off one of your ears, then at least do QE on the way to the emergency room.

Since creativity flows from Self, take time to get to know your Self. Increasing creativity is far more effective when Extended QE is performed. Five, ten, or even twenty minutes will help. With extended times there is no need to repeat your intention, but you may find your mind lazily examining the problem from different directions. Don't initiate this examination. Let it take its own course. Don't interfere; just watch. The solution may present itself slowly, but almost always it is revealed in a flash of insight and almost never how or when you expect.

If creativity doesn't arrive immediately, than the seed thought you dropped into the sea of pure awareness while floating on your Eufeeling is still germinating. It is organizing, rallying all the forces of creation around your concerns. The answer is coming; just wait and watch, whiling the time away with your Eufeeling. If it doesn't arrive in this session, take a break and do another session later.

This is a foolproof method of revving up the creative juices, but in the beginning it may take time mainly because your mind keeps trying to make something happen. I can guarantee your answer will come but never as expected, so lighten up and just hang out. If your answer did come as you expected, then you would not be creating anything, would you? So once you drop your question into the fertile soil of awareness don't bother with it again. Continually checking your intention is like digging up a seed every day to see if it is germinating. It will never grow if you continually disturb it. Just sit back and enjoy the delight of a day on the ocean of bliss.

When will creativity come? Sometimes it will arrive bundled in the light of recognition right away and sometimes later that day or the next. When you get good at not looking for an answer, it will come almost immediately.

When I write, I often get stuck for a word or how to lay out a concept in practical, comprehensible language. Most of the time, I find myself looking momentarily away from my monitor screen. I find my Eufeeling always waiting patiently for my recognition and the word or concept or answer comes quickly and completely.

For instance, the whole idea of thoughts being like arrows that should be drawn back to awareness sprung spontaneously from a brief sideward glance into nothing while the wheels of the mind stopped. The seed thought, "How can I explain what happens in the mind using the archery analogy?" Almost instantly I saw thoughts like darts shooting up from pure awareness, each one hitting the target dead center. Total time elapsed: four seconds.

Many times—especially when I am mentally fatigued from writing and my back is a little stiff from hours of sitting—I will shuffle across the living room to the couch and lie down. Sometimes I lie there for less than a minute when the puzzle pieces fit perfectly together and I march excitedly back to my computer eager to transform the concept into words. The only problem with this rapid turn-around is that my back is just starting to relax when I'm back to my seat.

Once I was wrestling with a particularly convoluted concept and stayed at my computer way too long before I decided to do it the easy way and found my way to the couch. I lay down with heaviness, looking for physical relief as much as a solution to my quandary. When I hit the cushions, fully expecting to linger at least for a few minutes, I bounced right back to my feet and returned to the keyboard because the solution had settled neatly in my mind. My ego has habituated to the release from conscious control and now actually enjoys the fruits of pure observation.

When to Plant the Seed of Creativity

The active mind is planting seeds all day long. We call them desires. If you listen to your mental chatter long enough, you will find it full of judgment and desire. On the superficial and weaker level of the conscious mind, many thoughts are directed at what we want and how to get it. That is because at that level we are isolated from awareness of pure awareness and look outward for fulfillment in things, people, events, and ideas. No matter how strong the desire at this level the action will be weak and fulfillment of the desire is not realized. Or it is realized only after a great deal of work and will power.

The mind settled in pure awareness has few desires other than those that are beneficial for all. The word desire is really too strong. These impulses are more like preferences. Rather than feeling, "I would really love to have that red sports car," the settled mind would think, "nice" and be able to enjoy it for what it is, without a need to own it. This approach saves on car payments, gas, and insurance. So right away many of the strong desires that your active mind has are satisfied simply by slipping below the waves of chaotic mental activity and dwelling in the depths of pure awareness.

If you are one who enjoys artistic activities like painting, music, writing, and dance, you are already familiar with being in the "zone." With QE, you can overcome those frustrating times when your art suffers from diminished creative flow. In writing, this is called writer's block. I've never had it. I sometimes get tangled up with how to say something or just don't feel like writing, but when I sit down, I can write. Why? I let the content flow from pure awareness through my Eufeeling and then "me" just records what is there. If you are in a creative slump, do QE daily and often and then become more active than usual. Walk or go dancing and then sit silently and do QE. You will be quite amazed at how your creative juices will begin flowing. You may need to carry around paper towels to soak up the excess juice.

If you are working on a math or engineering problem, the mechanics of creativity are the same. Become familiar with the particulars of the problem and then leave them for the quiet orderliness of Eufeeling. The annals of science and technology are fraught with examples of discoveries by individuals who found solutions to their problems while daydreaming or when just falling asleep. It was Friedreick Kekule, the discoverer of the benzene ring, who for months had been trying to figure out its molecular structure. He finally gave in and sat exhausted in his chair before the living room fireplace. His mind now free from imposed effort, he watched as the flames lazily curled and licked at the crackling logs. Then, in that silent state, the answer came to him. He watched as a flame curled around itself like a snake swallowing its tail. "Ah-ha," thought Kekule. "Benzene is a ring." And so it was.

It was in his quiet mind, settled in orderly stillness, that the answer took form and wriggled its way up into Kekule's disinterested conscious-ness. He was fortunate to have been sitting in front of that fire under those circumstances. You are far more fortunate. You have QE. You can visit pure awareness and wallow in the fullness of Eufeeling while the forces of life hasten to do your bidding.

So remember, when you come up against a stubborn problem of any kind, review the problem, then do QE. When you are aware of your Eufeeling, easily intend that the solution be forthcoming and then wait disinterested in that fullness for the answer to appear.

Helping Others

If others are having a creative crisis, you can help. Just have them think about what they want to accomplish and then you do QE. The best scenario may be an Extended-Remote QE session, but that is completely dependent on personal circumstances. Remote or other-wise, extended QE will probably be the fastest road back to free-flowing creativity. You will notice your own creativity opening as well.

Part II: The Body

Chapter 10

Healing Physical Pain

Today's need is not heroics but healing.

Warren G Harding

*At any one time your health is the sum total of all the impulses,
positive and negative, emanating from your consciousness.*

Deepak Chopra

To be able to heal the body with nothing more than pure awareness and a gentle touch might seem like science fiction but it is
an absolute certainty and it is literally at your fingertips. Quantum
Entrainment (QE) is an exciting innovation in human awareness that
stimulates rapid, deep healing in a matter of seconds to minutes. If you
are an athletic trainer, physiotherapist, massage therapist, or any professional used to traditional hands-on healing practices, get ready to be
amazed. If you are an M.D., D.O., E.M.T., chiropractor, acupuncturist,
nurse, or member of any of the healing arts, get ready to be amazed. If
you are an insurance adjuster, police officer, working mother, or anyone
else, get ready to be amazed. Why? Because QE is amazing.

Why is QE amazing? Because we believed our teachers, parents,
and peers when they told us that life is limiting. The QE process has
opened a chink in the armor of ignorance that has been fitted around
our imaginations. The ability to heal deeply and with intention has
always been ours. We were just taught otherwise. QE opens a new way

of thinking. Or more accurately, a new way of being for it is in being aware that all things become possible. The proof of the pudding, they say, is in the eating. And nowhere can the proof of healing awareness be recognized more profoundly than in the human body.

You are already human so you already have the "equipment" to heal physical maladies. The equipment I refer to is the ability to become aware of pure awareness. All humans do have this awareness, but you have something more that will permit you to heal right now. You already know QE. And in just a few minutes, with just a few pointers, you will be healing sprained ankles, headaches, back aches, tennis elbow, and stubbed toes. You are limited only by your imagination.

Before we start, let's orient ourselves to what is really happening when I say you "heal." When you perform QE and remove the symptoms of sciatica or reduce the swelling and bruising of a sprained knee, you are not really healing. You are doing QE and healing is getting done completely without your involvement. This is the only way it can work so don't start puffing up your chest and snapping your suspenders. The people in which you inspire a healing event will want to say you are a great healer but don't let them. You are Nothing, and that is the greatest compliment a human can be paid. We have taken credit for healing for centuries and you see where that has led us. So get out of your head and get out of the way. Do QE and let the healing chips fall where they may.

Here is an example of just how easy QE is to learn and how effective it can be even the first time you use it. Rick relates his story:

> Not long before hearing about QE, I noticed that one of my cervical vertebras (C3 or C4) was noticeably out of alignment. It felt like the transverse process was hovering above my right shoulder. Accompanying this was a pronounced vertigo while lying on my back and turning my head to the left—so intense that I felt like I was going to pass out. I was worried nobody would find me if I did.
>
> I downloaded the e-book and used myself as the subject. I placed my index fingers on the recommended places with the

intention "Perfectly aligned cervical vertebra, and free from vertigo." I did QE for only a couple minutes, then quit. Before I went to bed that night, I reached around and was surprised that my vertebra was noticeably closer to being centered! When I woke up the next morning, while still lying on my back, I checked again. My cervical vertebra was completely aligned, but I still had the vertigo when turning my head to the left. However, I was now acutely aware of a very sore spot at the base of my skull behind my left ear. Somehow, I instinctively knew this was the source of my vertigo. I did QE on that spot and I've not had any vertigo since then.

I've done QE with several friends and was pleased with how effective it can be. I've also had success with my daughter from a distance for the migraine headache she had.

Rick's experience is not unusual. I receive stories like this from all over the world. The incredible thing is that this potent hedge against pain is so natural to the human condition it can be learned from an e-book.

I'd like to mention just a word about doing QE on yourself. Some people have less success doing QE for their own problems than for other people's pain. The reason for this is that it is harder to get out of the way and let Self do its work when you work on yourself. What inevitably happens when we do QE for our own physical complaints is that we keep checking to see if it's working. Remember our seed analogy? The seed will never grow if you keep digging it up, and you will not heal if you keep looking for results. Just do QE and mentally walk away from it. Rick did QE on his vertebra and then went to sleep. You can't mentally walk much further away than that.

If you want to elicit a healing event for someone else, you simply point your consciousness in the desired direction and pull the pure awareness trigger. Let's say you call a friend and ask her if she wants to play a little tennis. She says that she can't because she just sprained her ankle walking off a curb. You say, "I'll be right over."

When you arrive, she is sitting with her ankle on a pillow propped up on a stool. The ankle is badly bruised and swollen. You ask her to stand and try and walk so you can see how badly the ankle is injured. She stands and juggles on her good leg for stability. Leaning on your shoulder, she gingerly places the heal of her damaged foot on the floor and tries to put a little weight on it. She yelps and recoils in pain and looks at you like you are a madman for asking her to walk on that foot. She sits down with a forceful sigh and a defeated look on her face. She places her ankle back on the padded stool.

You pull up another stool and sit next to her injured ankle, gently wrapping your hands and fingers around it and...what? You tell me. You already know. Do QE just like you learned in the first section of this book. That's it, that's all, end of story.

With your hands in place, find your thoughts and watch them until they slow down and stop. Then your Eufeeling will waft into your awareness. Easily be aware of your Eufeeling, or thoughts or the Nothing of pure awareness, whatever presents itself in your mind. While you are doing this, healing is taking place. That's right; in a matter of minutes, you will feel the swelling fall away under your fingers and the dark purple bruising begin to lighten. As you continue to observe your Eufeeling, your friend may feel an intensification of her symptoms. The pain and throbbing may increase for awhile but soon that will give way to relief. She will report that the throbbing ache is almost gone. She chances rotating her ankle and a look of surprise widens her eyes as she exclaims, "I can move it without pain. Look, the swelling is gone!"

You ask her to stand again and try and walk on her foot. She flashes you a brief look of incredulity which fades quickly as she rotates her ankle free of pain. You help her stand and she tentatively places her heel on the floor, puts a little more pressure on it, and then lays her foot down flat. Next she puts weight on the foot and begins to walk. Her walking is almost normal.

You tell her that the healing will continue for the next day or two all on its own and to use it as much as it feels good to do. She's not yet ready to play tennis, but she tells you that dinner is on her and you head out for sushi.

Your friend's ankle will heal remarkably fast with just one session of QE, but you can do subsequent sessions and the healing will be faster and deeper. Did you need to go running over to her house to perform QE? Of course not, because you know how to do Remote QE. QE works just as well at great distances as it does hands-on.

Let me ask you this: What was your intention? You didn't have one, right? You didn't need one because the intention was implied. You both knew what needed to be done so you didn't even have to consciously form it in your mind. Almost all of my QE sessions are free of conscious intention. I either don't know what my partner wants help with or she mentions it and I forget about it almost immediately. You don't have to formulate a clear intention. Pure awareness is pretty smart. It made you and everything in this world and beyond it. And it did all that without your help. Cool, huh?

I think it is obvious, but at this point I just need to say it. Always consult a duly licensed healthcare professional when circumstances demand it. Don't take chances with your, or anybody else's, health. One does not exclude the other. When you go to a doctor, also do QE. That way you are covering all your bases. If you have to take medication, QE will not only help the medicine do its job more effectively but it will also reduce or eliminate side effects caused by the drug. Be safe and play it smart.

CHAPTER 11

Improving Athletic Performance

The greater the emphasis upon perfection, the further it recedes.
Haridas Chaudhur

*Life is creative. It plays itself into existence, seeking
out new relationships, new capacities, new traits.
Life is an experiment to discover what's possible.*
Margaret Wheatley

I very much admire what athletes can do with their bodies. I've played sports all my life and love the feeling I get when I'm challenging my body to perform. I love working on a skill in practice only to witness as it is spontaneously and flawlessly expressed during competition. The athlete also has to maintain a highly tuned psychological game. I know the hardship it places on the psyche when a magnificent, athletic body is injured. Most athletic slumps are more mental than physical. Quantum Entrainment (QE) successfully addresses both mental/emotional and physical problems. And of course QE is invaluable for the completely healthy athlete as well.

Healing Athletic Injuries

I don't think we need to dwell too awfully long on QE's ability to heal physical complaints except to say that every athlete, professional, or recreational should know QE. QE really shines when it comes to soft tissue injury like muscle and ligament sprain/strain, spinal disc damage, and even nervous tissue repair. And the sooner QE is applied, the deeper and more quickly that injury will heal.

Imagine a football player who, early in the match, pulls a hamstring while running. He falls to the ground, rolls over, and grabs his upper leg in pain. Immediately, he becomes acutely aware of the pain and the thoughts that are swirling around the pain like angry bees around a smashed bee hive. Very soon his thoughts stop their frantic buzzing and begin to settle down. His Eufeeling pokes its head into his conscious-ness and the pain and cramping subside. He limps slightly as he leaves the field to sit on the bench. The team trainer places his hands on the player's upper leg and joins the football player in doing QE. A few minutes later he wraps the leg and has the player continue doing QE for himself. Twenty minutes after, he sends the player back on the field, free of any symptoms.

Does that sound crazy? It shouldn't. Our bodies have an extraordi-nary ability to heal—an incredibly remarkable ability to repair damaged tissues. The way we see healing today is so limited. Our vision of healing is pathetic and as long as we believe in that vision, it will remain pathetic. Our potential is eons ahead of what we are living but the astonishing thing is we don't have to evolve over generations into super-healing. We can do it today simply by turning our consciousness toward pure aware-ness. And the more of us who do, the more quickly others will abandon their beliefs to the contrary. Once their blinders fall away, not only will our bodies heal more effectively but so will our minds, emotions, rela-tionships, and environment. My goodness, what are we waiting for?

Here's an example of what I mean. My wife Martina is a European trained massage therapist and a large part of her practice is directed toward professional athletes. One morning she received a call from a tennis player who was warming up on the court when he injured his back. He described his symptoms and asked Martina if she could give him a therapeutic massage to help ease the pain. She said that she couldn't work on him in his acute condition but her husband had a special process that would help and she explained QE. He said no matter how "weird" it sounded, he would try anything to remove the deep pain he felt.

When we arrived at his condo, I recognized his antalgic posture to indicate a herniated disc. I performed enough of an orthopedic exam to confirm my first impression. Standing, he was bent forward and to the right at almost 45 degrees and he absolutely could not straighten up. He had his right hand on his bent knee for support and he could barely shuffle if I asked him to walk.

Many years in practice as a chiropractor told me it would take several days of bed rest and treatment to eliminate the pain and get him mobile enough for therapy. It would take several weeks to get him anywhere near a tennis court again. He confirmed my suspicion by telling me that this had happened twice before and he was laid up for several weeks each time. "This time was by far the worst," he told us. It had been a couple of hours since the injury so I started QE right away. While he stood bent almost in two leaning on his knee, I contacted his back and began. Three or four minutes later, I asked him to stand up straight. He looked at me as if I was from Mars and then looked at Martina as if to say, "What kind of madman have you let into my house?"

We both encouraged him to try and he started to work the hand he was leaning on for support slowly up his right thigh. At first he was very tentative, but he grew in confidence as his back straightened without increasing the pain. In fact, the straighter his back became, the bigger his eyes became. It was a thing of beauty to behold. Free of pain, he stood almost erect. I asked him to return to the bending position again and I did QE on him for a minute or two more and asked him to straighten up again. He did so with confidence and straightened all the way this time. We left him smiling broadly with instructions to take it easy until he was certain he could return to the court at which time he should make an appoint for athletic massage therapy. We got a call from him two days later from the tennis court where he was hitting a few warm-up balls without pain or restriction.

The value of QE for athletic injuries is unquestionable. QE is fast, effective, and non-invasive. It does not hurt to apply and cannot create any further insult to the injured tissue. It is perfect.

Improving Athletic Performance

What does it mean to improve athletic performance? It means to enhance coordination between body and mind. But what does coordination between mind and body mean? And why do we need a body in the first place? Silly question? Let's take a look.

Most of us live in a world that is not too physically challenging. We don't have to climb hills and trap game and throw spears to survive. We learn most of the survival motor skills when we're young, then coast the rest of the way. But athletes have chosen to up the ante by pushing their bodies, honing them into finely precision instruments.

Athletic performance starts in our mind. Our mind is the container for thoughts. We look outward into the world through our senses. Sensory impressions come into our mind, are processed, and then, if we decide to execute some necessary action, our body responds to fulfill that action. Of course, this is a gross oversimplification but it will do for our purposes here. Our mind is like the driver and our body is like the car. Our body is the vehicle for our consciousness. It drives it around so that our consciousness can experience through the senses and increase our relative knowledge of the world we inhabit. When consciousness is ego-driven, we are motivated by fear and can't really enjoy the ride. It's like driving in traffic when you think that every car is trying to hit you. When Self is in the driver's seat, the body/mind are relaxed and easily reactive. So it is with athletics. An athlete settled in the Self is also relaxed, and spontaneously responds physically. You will hear a Self-centered athlete say about their performance, "I was in the zone. My body performed flawlessly and I was perfectly calm."

When an athlete is Self-aware, they are fluid and free-flowing. They are less likely to injure themselves. They often feel as if their bodies are on automatic pilot. Playing Self-aware is an effortless delight and one of the greatest joys of life.

Many athletes turn professional for the wrong reasons. They see a chance to do what they love and get paid for it. But if they fail to cultivate Self-awareness outside the playing field, they will inevitably focus on fame or fortune and the joy of performing is soon lost. They burn brightly and then burn out. The softness of Self is traded for the hellish hard life of sharp edges and straight angles. QE will bring balance to an athlete's life, harmonizing his personal and professional life while it protects the joy that playing brings to his heart.

The following is a story of one such athlete. Julian Link has maintained his exuberance for life and his excitement for his sport in the very competitive and stressful arena of professional tennis. Julian is from Germany and plays in the 35 years and older league. But that was all threatened when he sustained a knee injury while playing fatigued under trying circumstances. Here is Julian's story in his own words:

> *I am a professional tennis player in the over-35 league. At the end of the year, I felt burned out and very tired. It was then that I hurt my knee playing tennis. I tore a ligament and couldn't touch the ground with that leg. I treated it with ice and anti-inflammatory drugs. After a week of treatment, the knee was no better and they wanted to do an MRI on it. That week I met Dr. Kinslow. He did a QE treatment on my knee for about five minutes and immediately I felt a little better. When I asked for more sessions, he told me that I would be able to do it myself. After reading a copy of his book, I started doing QE on my knee.*
>
> *After only a couple of days, I had the Eufeeling and was working on my knee. Every time I did QE, my knee felt better. I knew the knee was healing itself. I worked on the knee daily and after 40 days it was completely free of pain. Now I am playing in tournaments—and winning—and I have no problems with my knee at all.*
>
> *But there is a bigger benefit from working on my knee. Ever since I learned how to use QE, every part of my life has gotten better. I find immediate peace whenever I need it. Since I am a*

professional athlete, I heavily rely on an inner calm and peace in order to bring out the best in me. Since using QE, I am able to feel that flow nearly on a daily basis. But this summer I started having a fluid and flowing experience in me like never before. Playing tournaments I had an incredible peace and strength that let me reach new heights in my playing and joy inside.

Julian not only overcame the physical damage to his knee with QE but he also realized the joy of doing athletics when Self-aware could also be realized off the tennis court as well. As he continued to be Self-aware he found that QE improved his competitive edge astonishingly. In 2007 and 2008, Julian became European Champion and in 2008 he defeated the best player in the world in his age group.

Julian is living the vision I have for all athletes: Self-healing both in and outside of their athletic endeavors. But the vision goes beyond athletes. Whether we are athletes, computer wizards, CEOs, or welfare recipients, integrating QE into our lives must necessarily raise us above the struggling human condition and free us to be naturally who we are to do instinctually what we love to do.

CHAPTER 12

Space Walking

*Humanity's survival depends on all of our willingness
to comprehend feelingly the way nature works.*

Buckminster Fuller

*Nature! We are surrounded and embraced by her:
powerless to separate ourselves from her...She has neither
language nor discourse; but she creates tongues and hearts,
by which she feels and speaks...She is all things.*

Goethe

Walking is excellent for rejuvenating the body. Our beating heart and circulating blood infuses our tissues with energy-giving oxygen and removes the toxins that cause physical and mental discord. What most people don't realize is that walking can be an excellent exercise for our other heart—the one we often refer to as our soul or spirit. I call this space-walking, and the benefits go far beyond a traditional stroll in the park. Let me explain.

To the casual passerby space-walking looks the same as plain old everyday one-foot-in-front-of-the-other walking. But, inside the space-walker, the symphony of the spheres sings in perfect harmony with the sparrow's song; the wind through the grass; the beating of every heart of every created being. Sound impossible? Not at all. Space-walking is not only possible but it is also easy once you know how.

As we navigate through our daily routine, our senses remain engaged by things and our minds by thoughts. For instance, when we enter a room we note the things that occupy that room. We see the coffee cup on the table next to the couch on which Aunt Tilley is blissfully entangled in her afternoon nap. But there is something in the room of great value and it rarely gets noticed: space. That's right—simple, all-enveloping space.

When we pay attention to space instead of the objects that define it, something very magical begins to take place. Our minds slow down and our bodies relax. Then we begin to see our world in a most beautiful and wondrous way. Our lives are forever and incredibly enriched simply by acknowledging space. Here's why.

Both saints and scientists tell us that all things come from nothing. You remember David Bohm, a quantum mechanical theorist considered by Einstein to be one of the best in his field. He coined the phrase "implicate order" to indicate the nothing from which all creation is spun like the web from a spider. From the nothing comes the basic building block of life, the wave. Waves create particles and particles create atoms. Then atoms create molecules which then create stars and cars and candy bars. That's Creation 101 in a nutshell. Everything we see comes from primordial nothing.

When we become aware of nothing, we travel back to our birthplace as it were. Coming home nurtures both body and soul. It feels good and, as we will see in a moment, is so good for us.

Now space is not nothing. It is simply the emptiness between two objects. Space can contain air, radio waves, odors, dust mites, water vapor, and so on. But to the mind, space represents nothing so we can use space as our gateway to bliss and harmony. So now let's lace up our walking shoes and learn how to space-walk.

Start out with a gentle walk in pleasant surroundings. As you walk, begin to notice not birds or cars or plants but rather the space between these things. Find the space between the trees, between the branches and then locate the space between the leaves. Don't look at the clouds; look into the vastness between the clouds. Anywhere you see two things, note the space between them.

You can use sound to find space as well. Listen to the even fall of your feet on the ground, then find the silence, the space, between your footfalls. Listen to the distant whine of a siren. Listen intently until the siren finally fades into silent space. Space is everywhere. You only need to become aware of it to begin space-walking.

Are you getting the idea? Now you are ready for the final step. This is the most important part of space-walking. Once you find space, don't look at it as if it were just another object to be identified. Your mind will become quickly bored if all you do is identify space. The mind likes stunning vistas and juicy problems to sink its mental teeth into. Space is neither of these.

Here's the trick, the magic of finding your soul and filling your heart. Once you find space, peer intently into it as if it was a thick fog and you are waiting to see what will come out of it. Look into the depth and breadth of every space and pay close attention to not only what you see but also to what you feel. That's right. Find your Eufeeling in the space between two objects. It will melt your heart.

Here is an excerpt from an e-mail I got from Nancy, a new space-walker.

> *After our conversation this morning, I went out for a run. I was much more aware of my body during this run: the flow of it, the rotation of my upper body in combination with the easy movement of my lower body. I needed no warm-up. I just set out in an even light run. The movement was so majestic it brought tears to my eyes. The most profound phenomenon during this run was that all the animals I passed did not move away. The swan, the egrets, and the herons gently gazed at me as I passed them. Several times during this magnificent hour, I held back tears of joy. I noticed the air wasn't "just air"; it was a silky, living presence waving its way around me.*

Nancy was actually a space-jogger. Of course you can do space-walking with any activity like tennis, roller blading, or just sitting and watching Aunt Tilley enjoy the bliss of stolen sleep. It is the space between the moments of our lives.

If you remember, I had you do a little space-walking as part of learning Quantum Entrainment (QE). After you learned to hold Eufeeling sitting quietly with your eyes open, you then got up and walked slowly around the room examining objects. Even though you were focusing on the objects, your mind was filled with pure awareness and so you recognized that pure awareness was also vibrating in those various items. Observing the space is easier to begin with but as your mind becomes more infused with pure awareness, it will feel equally at home with space or substance.

Start space-walking slowly and become more active as you learn how to hold the silence within the space. Many people will actually do QE before space-walking. This has the advantage of reminding the mind of the space between thoughts. It is a short step from there to see and feel the space between things.

See how many activities into which you can introduce space-walking. Consider space-working or space-cooking or even space-brushing your teeth. Have fun with it, but do it often and in time it will become effortless. Then you will be the one "holding back tears of joy."

Helping Others

You can help others space-walk by going with them and describing what you are doing. Make sure they are quiet to begin with and keep idle chatter to a minimum or even start with a QE session at home before you venture out. If you really want to have fun, take a group out space-walking. Pure awareness is more easily realized in a group. Eliminating idle chatter in a group is almost impossible so have silent time followed by short discussion periods. Groups of 3–8 are good. If you have more than 8, break into two groups.

This exercise is especially valuable for children. If you take out a group of children, encourage them to talk about their experiences as they occur rather than waiting for a formal discussion period. Children naturally take to the spaces and may even teach you a thing or two about the joy of space-walking.

Part III: Relationships

CHAPTER 13

Sex, Love, and Universal Love

Love is not a mere impulse;
it must contain truth, which is law.

Rabindranath Tagore

At the start of sexual union, keep attentive on the fire in the
beginning, and, so, continuing, avoid the embers in the end.

Shiva Sutras

Love has been a topic of interest and concern since the first caveman bonked his mate on the head with his club and dragged her by the hair into his bungalow-sized cave. That is before she planted petunias and had him build a white picket fence. I say love but I could have as easily said sex, for the two words are often used interchangeably. I am not a psychologist, scientist, or talk show host, so I am no expert on love. But I have fallen in love a time or two and that should count for something. For what it is worth, I will now offer my two cents on the topic of sex, love, and Universal Love.

First, I would like to untangle the arms and legs of sex and love to see if, in fact, there is a difference between the two. Then I would like to contrast sex and love with Universal Love—the goal of every spiritual aspirant on the path to salvation.

Sex is one of our greatest primal drives. I don't think I can add much to the libraries of information that exist around this topic. Amazing

115

how such a simple, three-letter word can cause so much commotion. I teach Alternative Healing at Everglades University in city, state. When the collective consciousness of a class tends to wander away from the topic at hand, all I have to do is write "sex" on the board and within 2.35 seconds, I have every student's complete and undivided attention. As they say in the advertising business, "Sex sells."

Sex is biological. It is hard wired into our brains for the survival of our species. But there seems to be more to sex than a simple pleasure impulse designed to inspire us to repeat the process over and over until we populate the earth. In light of our present over population predicament, it is a shame we didn't come with some kind of reset button. But that is another story for another day.

Sex is an intricate part of falling in love. When we see someone who is attractive to us, our senses stimulate our brains to release sex hormones. We become sexually aroused and can be satisfied with just the physical release or we may feel all warm and fuzzy, the precursor to what many call love.

This warm, fuzzy "romantic love" can overwhelm us during the first few months of a new relationship. We may become consumed by the fires of love and while under its spell, make life-altering decisions like eloping and joining the circus as a husband and wife knife-throwing team. (Sorry, I didn't mean to dredge up my personal history.) Anyway, what I'm trying to say is that out of the physical act of sex, we humans tend to experience strong emotions for our partner. We collectively refer to these emotions as love. In fact, sex is a good barometer for how well a relationship is doing. When a relationship experiences difficulty, sexual intimacy is usually the first causality. On the other hand, when things are going very well between partners, thoughts of sex bound unbidden into our minds to quickly find fruition in our bodies. There they stay until the desire is again doused by the doldrums of daily living.

When the emotions of a new love wash over us, we feel like it will never end. We think that we will always feel this way about our partner. But, as anyone who has fallen in love can attest, that "new love" feeling doesn't last. That incredible, bombastic, rocket ride into the wobbly world of love just doesn't last; it can't. And here is why it can't.

Romantic love, whether born of sexual union or not, is conditional love. In fact, the term "making love" infers that we perform sexually and then love is produced. Love is a condition of sexual union. But there are many other aspects to romantic love. It depends on many circumstances like beauty, form, functionality, and any traits that trip psychological triggers that, when triggered, we can hear ourselves say, "I don't know why I love him; I just do." The poets and songwriters never tire of extolling the virtues of this lofty love. They might say, "Her hair is the golden light of morning, her eyes soft, luminescent pools of compassion, and her smile fills me with the radiance of life." Or simply, "I like the way she walks. I like the way she talks."

Conditional love waxes when our partner does loving things and wanes when they don't. Isn't it true? The first blast of bliss is slowly replaced by the complacency of a more practical love with time and circumstance. Stress, anger, resentment, discouragement, anxiety, fear, desperation, depression, and emotional over-reaction all weaken our ability to love. Despite the loftiest of intentions, love embers slowly cool and in over 60% of our relationships, if government statistics are accurate, dies. At this point, the drained relationship continues out of convention or it ends and we go eagerly off in search of another partner to fill the empty space vacated by conditional love.

Here is the point. Conditional love is inspired or caused by something: holding a child, caring for a pet, selflessly giving of yourself, caressing a lover, exercising, praying, meditating, etc. We humans are capable of performing a plethora of actions that create chemical changes in the body and increase feelings of love. That makes love conditional. There is a spiritual saying that speaks to this condition of conditionality. It goes, "What you will get, you will lose." We gain love for a reason and we lose love for a reason. Conditional love is tied to conditions and conditions are always changing. What is born will die. Love born of conditions is born to die.

But there is a deeper love that underlies conditional love. We can never recapture the intensity of the first few months of a new love for one single and simple reason. We are meant for something far more fulfilling and important than conditional love. This love is unconditional. It is universal. It is the foundation for all spiritual pursuits and yet cannot be gathered in by the efforts of even the most adept devout aspirant. It is practical and primordial. It is Universal Love.

Universal Love has no gender. It belongs neither to man nor woman nor to the union between them. Some say it is of the heart, soft and filled with adoration. It is said that if you love deeply enough, you will transcend carnal love, merging with Universal Love. This thinking is often referred to as the devotional path to enlightenment. Enlightenment is another word for living Universal Love. But I see a red flag whenever a path to universal anything is suggested. If something is universal, like unbounded love, then it must be everywhere all the time, right? If Universal Love is everywhere, where could you possibly go to get it? Wherever you are, there it is. A path can't take you to where you already are. We know this.

You see, Universal Love is already there waiting for you if you know how to embrace it. We don't need a path or a process. We just need to become aware of where we are, right? That is because Universal Love is also where we are. The whole problem of being in Universal Love is not so much a matter of doing something as it is a matter of *not* doing something. Not doing allows the dust and clutter of our minds to settle out. What happens when the mind settles down? Viola, Universal Love!

The real purpose of a loving relationship is not to fall more deeply in love with the other person. The purpose is simply to become aware of Universal Love. As we have seen, romantic love ebbs and flows with the tides of condition. While the promise of conditional love is an illusion, the promise of Universal Love does not exist at all. That's right. Universal Love does not promise anything. It already is complete as it is, at this very moment. It couldn't be otherwise or it wouldn't be universal. All we lack is the realization that this is so. Once done, we are done, and the perfection of the present is realized in all its mundane beauty.

Once we become aware of Universal Love, sex and conditional love still remain a part of our everyday world but with one very monumental difference. Anchored in Universal Love, sex and love and family; and finances, life and death are no longer separate events. They become part of a symphony. They are notes played on the background melody of Universal Love. Each note, by itself beautiful, adds to the wholeness of the piece. If we know only individual notes, we miss the harmony of the work. Becoming aware of Universal Love, we become aware of the melody behind the madness of conditional living. And, becoming aware of Universal Love is easy, effortless

QE effortlessly elicits awareness of Universal Love. Once thought refines and finally dies away, it is reborn as Eufeeling, the first glimmer of Universal Love. In time and with practice, you will be able to recognize your Eufeeling in every aspect of your relationship, including physically sharing love with your partner. Eufeeling awareness adds the missing element to love, broadening and deepening its meaning and intensifying its physical expression. This is how sex and love find fullness in Universal Love. This is where humanity realizes its divine spark. This is where love becomes Love.

CHAPTER 14

The Perfect Relationship

Where "my" and "your" stop, love begins.

Karl Renz

A loving heart is the beginning of all knowledge.

Thomas Carlyle

In the Beginning...

...was the word...and the word was Love; unconditional, boundless Love. Then, in Love, the One created the many. Love was frozen into form and creation was born. That Wholeness splintered into infinite expressions of Itself. Each splinter separate, yet whole. Love saw the multitudes and called them Self. Each Self appeared outwardly unique, but all were woven from the same all-permeating essence. From the faintest subatomic shiver to the silent power of revolving galaxies, the cosmos was filled with the infinite, flawless expressions of Self.

In the Present...

...our world, your world, is crammed full of things. Every thought and emotion, friend and foe, mountain, mosquito, and slice of cold pizza is the complete expression of Self born of Love. The problem is that most of us don't see it that way. We see the pieces but miss the Love waiting within. Let's look at love and Love from a little different perspective than we did in the last chapter. Let's consider conditional love as "me" and universal love as Self.

When we meet someone and fall in love, what is really happening? That depends on the kind of love we have fallen into. Love comes in two apparent forms: "me" love and Self love. "Me" is everything that makes a person unique. "Me" is made of thoughts and emotions, experiences, memories, hopes and fears. "Me" love is conditional love and changes as conditions change.

Self is the unchanging part of you that was there in childhood, adolescence, and is there now, never interfering but supporting all that you are. Your Self is your expression of Love but is not limited to you. Your Self, the Self of others, and even the pizza delivery dude that transported the cold pizza to your door are all one. The love of Self knows unity in diversity. It is unconditional.

Self loves without reason and "me" looks for reasons to love. When we "fall in love," it is "me" that does the falling. New "me" love is fiery and all-consuming; and doomed to mediocrity. Why? Why does it always happen that way? No matter how long the relationship lasts, we never recapture the sheer power of the first days of love.

When we believe in the "me" image of ourselves, we separate us from what we perceive as other images and we miss the unifying Love within. I do not see you as you really are. I see you as my mind wants to see you. While I am creating an image of "you", you are busy creating an image of me. We are like two puppeteers, each feverishly working our own puppet. So engrossed are we in making the puppets relate, we never get to know the other puppeteer.

Krishnamurti told us that relationships are formed between two images that the mind has created. He further revealed that the two images have their own needs and desires. They have their own agendas and live virtually isolated, within their separate worlds, taking comfort in the illusion of agreement. Krishnamurti said "... the images run parallel, like two railway lines, never meeting, except, perhaps, in bed ... What a tragedy it has become."

Most of us enter into a relationship for a reason like love or friendship, protection, money, excitement or danger, intellectual stimulation, or physical pleasure. Then, is the purpose of forming a relationship solely for gain?

Yes! The answer to the question, "Why do relationships exist?" is that they do so solely for gain. But they do not exist solely for our selfish gain, quite the contrary. Relationships are not strengthened by more money, control, or time. They are not even justified, as is commonly thought, by increasing the intensity of love between two people. Eckhart Tolle hit it right on the button when he said, "A rela tionship is to make you aware—not happy." Relationships are perfect opportunities to become Self-aware.

The flirtatious conditional love cannot last. We cannot live the illusion of conditional love when Universal Love is only a heartbeat away. Our Self will not allow it. Something will always go wrong. When it does, we wake up. After awakening, we usually try and fix the apparent problem. The waking up is good; it is the fixing that is misguided. Trying to fix a "me" relationship just leads to more problems that need to be fixed. Isn't that your experience? You can't fix an illusion with an illusion.

The real problem is the illusion that the relationship needs to be fixed. We want to make things right when the truth is, *they already are*. This is not a case of the glass being half full or half empty. This is a fundamental and profound shift in our perception. This is where "me" awareness grows into Self-awareness. Perfect Love created every Self in perfect harmony with every other Self. Simple awareness of this simple state yields complete freedom to Love.

Our part in a relationship is, to take responsibility for our own awareness. The rest will take care of itself. This is a leap of faith for many. Our partner doesn't need to stop his annoying snuffling or her continuous chatter. We need to be aware. That is all. That is how simple it is. The perfect relationship starts and ends with awareness of Self. When Self-awareness dawns, the two "railway lines" meet, not on the horizon, but at our very feet, and Love shimmers on the surface of every Self.

Quantum Entrainment (QE) exposes conscious awareness to Self. QE gently disengages consciousness from the playthings that litter our playground world and allows it to settle on Self as gently as a butterfly on the petal of an exotic flower. Relationships are all around us. We form relationships at the office, the grocery store, at the doctor's office. No matter how they fare in the particulars, all of them are perfect relationships when we have fallen in love with our Self.

Helping Others

If your spouse or significant other is being a bit of a pain (and we don't have to go into specific details here), then QE can help. In this case, you will help them to get through their discomfort remotely. Remember, you don't have to have their consent to do QE for them. But the most important and effective help you can provide for them is to do QE for yourself. Your change will greatly inspire change in them.

Part IV: Everything Else

CHAPTER 15

Sleeping and Insomnia

Sleep is the best meditation.

Dalai Lama

Sleep, the most beautiful experience in life...except drink.

W.C. Fields

Falling asleep is a natural, beautiful process. I say natural because when conditions are prime, you only have to lie down and do nothing and sleep comes. I like activities that involve doing nothing. When mastered, sleeping makes you feel great. You have more energy, think more clearly, and look better (at least some of us do).

Here's a hint for those of you who sleep pretty well but want to get a little more rest out of a night's sleep. When you get into bed, just before lying down, do Quantum Entrainment (QE) for 2–5 minutes. It is a wonderful way to wash away the superficial stress gathered during the day. It allows your body to throw off those tiny knots it is been tying all day and puts your mind in neutral, resetting your internal sleep meter to aaahhhhh! Then lie down and drift into the heavenly bliss of deep sleep.

For many people, however, sleeping is hard to do. I used to be one of those people, but now I sleep like a baby. (Maybe that's not the best comparison as any bleary-eyed parent of a newborn baby can tell you.) There are all kinds of reasons people don't sleep well—like consuming stimulants, eating poorly, and not getting enough exercise. Jet lag, hormonal imbalance, and other medical conditions, such as pain or mental/emotional stress, can also interrupt sleep patterns. The list is a long one and it doesn't seem fair that something so vital and enjoyable as a good night's sleep can be so easily disturbed. Insomnia is a symptom, and if you are sleeping poorly, make sure you find out why and then fix it. If you drink too much caffeine, then cut back. If you need more exercise, then get off the couch and walk around the block. If you can't fix the problem or even find out what it is, then it's time for QE.

One of the most common causes of sleeplessness is emotional stress. Sometimes you will know exactly what is bothering you and sometimes you won't have a clue. QE works beautifully in both cases. Since QE works to harmonize your whole being, it is perfect at getting into those hard-to-reach corners of your mind where undiscovered stress hides. For general stress, I recommend you do QE throughout the day. You can do it a minute at a time or for longer periods as much as 10 to 30 minutes. My favorite time for extended QE is first thing in the morning. It really sets the tone for the day. Done just before bed, I believe QE helps balance hormonal activity including melatonin secreted by the pineal gland regulating your internal night/day clock.

Getting to sleep and staying asleep can be a real problem—especially when something is bothering us. Maybe you had a fight with your boss or are struggling with the bills. Or perhaps your teenager just got a tattoo of all the members of her favorite heavy metal band up both arms, around the neck, culminating in the grand finale with the drummers crossed sticks perfectly aligned in the center of her forehead. She says she'll love them forever. And you wonder why sleep eludes you.

Stress can kick the mind into overdrive. Thoughts blur like the whirring blades of a fan, and we hear ourselves begging for just a few minutes of blessed mental silence. Now is the perfect time for QE. QE quiets thought simply by observing it. You have already experienced the no-thought state of pure awareness and how thoughts softly gather around your Eufeeling. This will work in times of stress as well, but differently.

When you are in the thick of a stressful event and you do QE, you will find the experience somewhat different than when you are more settled. It is all very relative. When your thoughts rattle like machine gun bullets on a tin roof and you begin QE, you might find that your machine gun thoughts punch holes in your awareness. Your thoughts run away with your awareness and QE is forgotten sometimes for many minutes. If this happens, that is just fine. Even though you don't feel as settled as at other times, a great amount of healing is taking place. You will see that you will recover from the incident far more quickly than you otherwise would have even if you don't feel settled. In QE, we take what we get. It will always be far better than if we hadn't done QE.

What you don't want to do is make feeling peaceful a goal. As you already know, this creates a polarity which pulls you in two different directions. Yes, it's great to feel peaceful and free of discomfort, but working in the direction of peace is still working and that is opposed to peace. All that is needed is simple observation. Watch and wait. When you turn off the electricity to a spinning fan, it still takes time for the whirring blades to slow down and stop. And so it goes when you do QE in the midst of great agitation. Emotional stress is like the electricity that spins your thoughts. QE turns off the stress, but it takes time for the whirring thoughts to slow and stop. Just do your QE with no expectations and you will be really amazed.

Of course, doing QE while you are not agitated or under pressure is money in the bank. Then when the stress hits the fan, you'll only be inches from pure awareness and the soothing influence of your Eufeeling.

Helping Others

QE can truly help others get a good night's sleep, sometimes in just a few minutes. If you share a bed with a restless sleeper, just reach over and place your hand on his forehead, chest, or back and do QE. It won't be long before his breathing becomes deep and regular. Even if he doesn't fall sleep right away, he will get a deep rest just from the QE. Of course, QE is made to order for helping people suffering from lack of sleep due to illnesses.

Children who have a hard time settling down to sleep or who wake with nightmares respond exceptionally well to a gentle session of QE. When you are comfortable with the QE process for yourself, you can even read the little ones a bedtime story while you do QE.

CHAPTER 16

Good and Poor Eating Habits

From food are born all beings, which being born, grow by food.
All beings feed upon food, and when they die, food feeds upon
them.

Taittiraya Upanishad

When your stomach disputes you, lie down
and pacify it with cool thoughts.

Satchel Paige

Most people usually pay little attention to eating. We look on it as a necessary activity that is pleasant enough but many times takes us away from other activities like work. In the U.S., we tend to eat on the run, gulping down mouthfuls of burgers and burritos, steering with our knees while careening through rush hour traffic. We tend to focus mostly on the quantity and convenience of food rather than quality, ambience, and the actual process of digestion.

Nutritionists maintain that most diseases and conditions of the body are caused by, or complicated by, poor digestion. "Well," you say. "I don't have any control over my digestion. I swallow my food and digestion takes place automatically." Well, I'm here to tell you that you do have a good deal of control over your digestion and Quantum Entrainment (QE) can play a pivotal part in the process.

First of all, digestion begins in the mouth. Chewing and mixing

129

your food with enzymes starts the digestive process. Also chemical messages are sent from receptors on the tongue to the brain, telling it about the kind of food in your mouth. Your brain tells your stomach to prepare for food.

A lot goes on in the mouth, and chewing is a very important part of digestion and assimilation. If you don't break food down to almost liquid status, it may not be properly digested and cause all kinds of problems from allergies to eczema to fatigue to arthritis to emotional disorders and so on.

I have a habit of watching people eat. I know it's a little weird but the physician in me seems to come out in restaurants. I am forever surprised at how little chewing goes on. I will watch a diner take a full bite of burger, cheeks bulging, chew three or four times, then raise their chin toward the ceiling and swallow. You can actually see the congealed mush of wilted lettuce, pickles, white bread, and meat chunks work its way down the gullet like the vanquished prey of a boa constrictor. My, what we do when we choose not to chew.

So, how can QE help with eating and digestion? QE creates balance. A proper functioning digestive system, like every system of the body, must be in balance to function free of malady. Doing QE for 30 seconds before you eat will set the tone for your meal. It'll slow you down so that your digestive system can prepare for the meal to come. It will encourage you to chew your food longer and more slowly. But if you don't seem to be able to remember to take 30 seconds before a meal to do QE, then just do it as you are preparing to eat. Become aware of your Eufeeling and then allow your mind to think about the meal to come. If you like, you can add an intention that the food will nourish and support your body/mind in every way needed.

If you have a digestion-related condition, do QE any time. For instance, if you've finished your meal and your gall bladder has left you bilious and nauseous, reach for a handy-dandy bottle of QE. You will be amazed. Symptoms like nausea, burning, and gas can be quelled in seconds to minutes. I had a client whose stomach blew up like a balloon every time he ate. It was accompanied with pain and gas and the symptoms kept him from enjoying a dinner out on the town. The first time we did QE, it took several minutes for its effects to be noticed. But slowly, at first, and then more rapidly, you could actually see his distended stomach melt like butter on a warm skillet. As his tummy got smaller and smaller, his smile got bigger and bigger. Mine, too: no more gas.

He learned QE and now does it for himself. His condition is improving remarkably and so is his state of mind. Now he goes out to eat whenever he wants, enjoying both food and friendship.

QE affords not only a deep, healing rest for your body but also exerts a harmonizing influence over your emotions as well. Emotions like anxiety and anger have a negative impact on your digestive system. QE balances emotions that seem to have an effect on eating and digestion. A quiet mind is paramount for both effective digestion and assimilation.

Just because we eat something does not mean that the nutrition contained within that food will be assimilated into our cells. Eating while in a hurry or emotionally agitated has a devastating effect on whether or not nutrition reaches our cells. Eating under stress can cause ulceration of the stomach lining, constipation or diarrhea, gall bladder and pancreas problems, torsion of the bowls, inflammation of the pockets and folds of the intestines (diverticulitis) and so much more.

Although it is often overlooked, eating is extremely important to our overall health and productivity. We usually think of nutrition as something good for our bodies, but our minds, emotions, and even our social interactions are affected profoundly by what and how we eat and how it is digested and assimilated. I strongly suggest doing QE before a meal, during the meal, after the meal, or all three. What have you got to lose but a little dyspepsia?

Helping Others

First of all, a quiet dining partner will go a long way toward helping someone calm down while they are eating. If the person you are eating with is shoveling down food as if he were in a contest at the county fair and if he is are not open to doing QE himself, than your QE will help him to slow down. Even though QE is not an energy technique, QE creates wells of positive, soothing energy around anyone who does it. This soothing energy will work its way across the dinner table to quiet the offending diner. During the course of the meal, he will quiet down and act more appropriately. If you find his obnoxious behavior is not responding fast enough, then just get up, walk around the table, place your hand on his forehead, and do QE. This behavior on your part is guaranteed to get him to stop eating, if only momentarily, but he will get the point.

By the way, the more aware one is of pure awareness, the more peace she generates. But don't be fooled by thinking that peace is a barometer for awareness; it isn't. The Bhagavad-Ghita, an ancient text that poses and answers all the general problems facing humankind, warns that we can never tell how evolved someone is by observation of outward appearances or how we feel in their presence. However, insufferable behavior at the dinner table is a pretty good indication of lack of awareness.

Of course, you can also help others by doing QE to help their poor eating habits and symptoms improve. You do not need to get permission to do QE for anyone, anytime. That is because you are not doing anything. You are only becoming aware of awareness and watching to see what happens. Your intention will not work if it is, in any way, harmful to that person or to the environment. You are safe to QE your little heart out on anything you like. In fact, I encourage it.

CHAPTER 17

Effortless Travel

It is better to travel well than to arrive.

Buddha

Though we travel the world over to find the beautiful,
we must carry it with us or we find it not.

Ralph Waldo Emerson

Some people find traveling fun while others find it inconvenient or even terrifying. Let's look at all three, in turn, to see how Quantum Entrainment (QE) can help make travel more fun, fulfilling, and effortless. While I will focus first on traveling by airplane, any of the QE tips for air travel can be applied to travel by car, boat, train, foot, donkey, and ostrich, to name a few. If you enjoy air travel, or at least tolerate it because it gets you where you want to go quickly (most of the time), then here are a few QE tips to make the event easier and more fun.

If you are traveling across time zones, you are open to the phenomenon called jet lag. Jet lag is a disruption of your circadian rhythms, which are regulated by a tiny area of your brain in your hypothalamus called the suprachiasmatic nucleus. Now, you can take that information and stuff it in your ear for all the good it will do you, but I thought I'd show off my ability to Google "circadian rhythms."

I do know this: when I travel by air—especially across time zones—I QE most of the time. For the most part, I don't read, engage fellow passengers in conversation, or look out the window until I've had my fill of QE. I just love the quiet and peace and full feeling I get QE-ing while traveling, but the real bonus is when I reach my destination more refreshed and, after a stretch and a yawn, am ready to take on the world. How does QE help reduce the effects of jet lag? Well, here's what I think.

Every 50 miles there is a change in the forces, for lack of a better word, that govern that region of Earth. We are becoming more aware of these subtle forces of nature—the vibrations and vortices that influence the subtle realms beyond our senses. While western science has not mapped them out with any certainty, eastern cultures and animals are very attuned to their presence.

Animals are at home with these electromagnetic and subtler force fields and use them to guide their activities. Birds fly thousands of miles along magnetic grids without getting lost. Animals know when there is abhorrence in the energy fields. If we know what to look for in their behavior, we can tell when a storm or earthquake is coming. My wife and I have a little white Shih Tzu named Daisy who will often bark at the front door five minutes before I get home. Likewise, if you watch children, you can tell when the ice cream truck is coming. (While this is not news for parents, I thought the rest of you would like to know so you don't chance missing the ice cream guy.)

My Transcendental Meditation teacher Maharishi Mahesh Yogi taught us that these forces he called "devas" influence the way energy manifests in a given part of our world. "Every 50 miles or so," Maharishi explained, "the influence of one deva yields to the influence of the next deva and so it goes all over the Earth." Growing up in one place sets your body/mind in harmony with those local laws. This is why you feel at home when you return to where you grew up.

When I was studying to become a teacher for the deaf, I learned that a good linguist could place a person within 50 miles of where they grew up just by listening to their speech patterns. These local laws of energy mold our minds and bodies and speech to be unique to that area. I had always wondered how the first English settlers speaking proper English could have ended up with a thick New York accent or the long, smooth drawl of those colonists inhabiting Georgia.

When you travel beyond your home deva's influence, your body is under more stress to adapt to the new energies affecting it. If you are walking, your body has time to adapt to the new laws. Traveling by car puts more demand on your body/mind to adapt to the quickly fluctuating subtle energies. Traveling by air has a much greater destabilizing effect as you pass through these energetic areas of influence. They tug and pull so quickly your body/mind is continually kept off balance. Flying across time zones adds the additional stress of perverting your circadian clock.

Doing QE while you fly, and to a lesser extent while you drive, will keep you in relative harmony with the local laws as they go whooshing by. Being aware of pure awareness creates a kind of superconducting frictionless flow that allows stress to pass around and through you without interfering with the normal functioning of your nervous system, cell metabolism, or thought processes. Traveling still takes effort and energy, but at least you are not creating harm by breaking the laws of nature. Doing QE while you pass through each deva's domain is kind of like having your passport in order so you don't get hung up at customs.

If flying causes you anxiety, then QE is made for you. Have a good long Emotional QE session before you leave for the airport, while waiting to board, and all the while you are on the plane. Remember, do not turn away from your fear but look at it easily while you are aware of pure awareness. Peace or stillness or some other manifestation of your Eufeeling will grow in your awareness and anxiety and fear will fall away.

If you become air sick, then QE will help there, too. You may initially find that the nausea will get stronger for few minutes. Stay with it as healing is taking place and soon you will be able to control the nausea with awareness alone.

When traveling by car, QE can be a great comfort. I rarely drive with the radio on. I love the silence and find pure awareness a friendly and supportive passenger. And not once has it told me that I'm driving too fast or that I just missed a prime parking spot like a wife I know. (Not you, honey. I was thinking of another wife who does that.) Get used to driving aware. Once you break the "gotta have sound" habit and turn off the radio, you will love the fullness of silence that surrounds you.

Speaking of parking spaces, try QE when looking for a parking space or when caught in traffic. Just have the easy intention for a clear space or for the traffic to yield to your intention and then forget about it from there. More often than not, you'll be surprised at how your Eufeeling works things out for you.

Helping Others

When you know QE, helping others travel makes it easier for them and fun for you. Of course, you will have to be on the lookout for excuses to don your cape and tights and appear as QE Man to save the day. The most common problems noted in an airport, for instance, are travel fatigue, irritability, and the "I'm late, I'm late, for a very important date" syndrome. You can help fellow travelers you don't know with Remote QE. You can do the same for family and friends by light touch or remotely if you like. Are the kids getting a little restless? QE! Have to go the restroom but can't get out of your seat? QE! Hungry, bored, or sick? QE, QE, QE! Just think QE first and then everything else. QE always helps, never hurts, and feels so good.

Chapter 18

Overcoming Financial Woes

*Money will come if we seek first the Kingdom of God
—the rest will be given.*

Mother Teresa

*The glow of one warm thought is to me
worth more than money.*

Thomas Jefferson

Money: a boon and a bane. Money has the power to light up man's mind and ignite his passions. It symbolizes both charity and lust, good and evil. When we have enough, we invariably want more. Rarely do we need it. At the very least, affairs concerning money are disruptive either in the acquiring it or its spending. Money is stored energy. Money, money, money, money, money. Could there be a more tantalizing topic?

As I write this chapter, the world's financial picture is not a rosy one. People the world over are experiencing financial hardship. Multimillionaires have lost their fortunes and the average wage earner is struggling to keep his head above the sea of debt that threatens to wash over him. Financial concerns are demanding a great deal of mental energy and there is much anxiety and even fear surrounding the individual, national, and world financial condition.

A financial concern almost always has two parts to it: 1) the actual logistics of the problem, and 2) the worry or fear that the mind attaches to that trouble. Quantum Entrainment (QE) can be applied to both. Let's discuss the second part, emotional attachment, first.

We already learned that fear is born of duality. That is, ego separates from awareness of pure awareness and sees the world as separate from its Self. It must fight alone against the infinite perceived threats to its existence. I say perceived threats because a change in perception can transform a foe into a friend. For example, if you find a coworker you thought was your friend acting suspiciously, whispering to other coworkers behind your back, then ending the conversation when you approach, you may have negative thoughts about their intentions. That is right up until the time that you open the door to the conference room and everyone yells, "Surprise!" and "Congratulations on your promotion." In the time it takes to exhale, your dubious coworker has become your best friend. You see, it is all a matter of perception, and perception follows awareness.

If ego has lost awareness of pure awareness, then its perception is one of deficiency. Desire for more than we really need is due to ego's misguided search for the ultimate treasure: pure awareness and its reflection in the mind the Eufeeling. Anchored in pure awareness the ego is fully expanded and feels no need for more money, more power, or more love.

When we perceive a lack of money, we also feel fear or one of its subservient emotions like anxiety, frustration, and anger. Obviously feeling fear will not resolve the problem of low funds. In fact, it makes the problem worse by creating mental and physical stress and interfering with more reasonable attempts to resolve the problem.

Fear all by itself can create a problem where there is none. We may fear that we will lose money or possessions or even loved ones even when there is very little chance of it happening. QE works beautifully and quickly to relieve fear born of financial difficulties. It pays off the ego's debts in the only currency it truly understands: pure awareness. Just that quickly, fear is replaced by peace.

Following is a testament by a woman living in Austria who was almost paralyzed by the fear of her financial predicament. I first taught her QE and then did a Remote QE session with her. Here's what she had to say about the session:

Worries about money had been a part of my life for a long time. Then one day, I had the chance to experience a combination Knowledge/QE session with Dr. Kinslow on this theme. In the first step, Dr. Kinslow asked me to bring up all the emotions associated with my fear about not having enough money. On a scale from 0–10 I had a 10+.

After that he taught me how to do QE for myself. After just a few minutes of practice, I again tried to bring up all the emotions that go with my financial worries. When I did, I was very happy and surprised. The emotions felt so far away that I couldn't even bring up these old feelings. They have stayed away since that time.

Then Dr. Kinslow did a Remote QE with me. We worked on a solution for my poor financial condition. After the Remote QE session, I had the deep feelings of peace instead of old fears and worries. Now I feel deep trust and I am not worried about money. A huge change has happened. Thank you so much!

Well, that was easy. Without effort, QE alleviates what is most often the worst part of financial difficulties: debilitating emotions. Now, let's turn to the actual circumstances that have created the loss of revenue.

Here we don't have to attend to particulars. We'll let the manifestation of pure awareness through the lens of Self do that for us. The hardest part of doing QE with a particular result in mind is to be able to let go of that perceived outcome in our mind. It seems counter-intuitive to just step back, wait, and watch as forces seemingly maneuver against us and circumstances unfold. But that is how it is done. Waiting and watching only seems counter-intuitive to a mind eager to manipulate circumstance in its favor. So you have a choice. You can use the limited resources of your individual mind, which is motivated by fear of failure, or you can do QE and let Self draw from the infinite resources of creation while centered in peace. So, are you ready to take the plunge into Nothing?

Sit in a comfortable chair where you won't be bothered for 5–10 minutes. Do QE and enjoy your Eufeeling. Become very aware of your Eufeeling. When you become more aware, it feels like your Eufeeling is getting stronger. But the Eufeeling is always perfectly strong. It is only how clearly you are aware of your Eufeeling that determines how strong it feels.

Once your awareness is very clear and your Eufeeling feels quite full, have a very simple intention poised in the present. Use something uncomplicated and positive—like "financially free" or "fulfillment of financial goals." Don't get greedy. If you do it right, Self will give you far more than you expect. You might even imagine yourself doing something you like that indicates that you are free of money worries. However you do it, do it simply and without expectation. Have fun with it. If fear and anxiety won't allow it, then do QE on the attached emotions.

Now, the hardest job is staying out of the way and waiting to see how Self will arrange for the payoff. That doesn't mean you don't work to get out of debt. You must do what is necessary. After the silence of Self comes the dynamic activity of its expression in your life. Do what seems right, but keep open to new and unlooked for opportunities. You may be offered unusual and even bizarre prospects. Look them over rationally. If they do not offer a workable solution, then they may lead to one. This is how Self works. Be ready. Looking back, you will marvel at the road taken. It will be easier and more exciting than the one you had planned...and far more successful.

I can add a personal note here. Two years before this writing, I was laid off from my work. I had a very, very large debt and the prospects for finding work for an old fogy like me were pretty poor. I was destitute and depressed—the perfect case for QE. One month after being laid off, I developed QE and began to test it on myself and others. One of the first things I worked on was my financial condition. Four months later, I wrote *The Secret of Instant Healing* and I QE'ed that the book would sweep the world helping all to learn this remarkably powerful healing process. Now, as I write the follow-up to *The Secret of Instant Healing*, I realize that every seed I planted in the early days of QE has germinated and are beginning to blossom fully. There is no way in heaven or hell that I could have worked this out by myself. Looking back, I am amazed at the convoluted path, the unforeseen gifts and kindness of strangers, not to mention the plain old dumb luck that it took to realize my intent. The moment I started was also the end. I was able, for the most part, to stay out of the way and let my Self work. When I took control, I only served to create effort and stress and slow down a process that was well oiled and running smoothly. Now you have the technology, the simple and sweet truth for realizing your deepest desire. That is, to be free of desire wrapped in the benevolent arms of your Self.

Helping Others

With QE you can help people with both parts of financial difficulties: the *emotional* and the *practical* hurdles. The emotional work is explained in detail in Chapter 8, *Healing Negative Emotions*. To work on the specific condition surrounding a person's financial concerns, have her use the intentions I've mentioned or you can use them for her. Remember not to be too complete or complex. Pure awareness likes it simple.

CHAPTER 19

Children

*The pursuit of truth and beauty is a sphere of activity in which
we are permitted to remain children all our lives.*

Albert Einstein

*The most interesting information comes from children,
for they tell all they know and then stop.*

Mark Twain

Sweet Little Martina and the Mean Old Ogre

Once upon a time there was a busy little village nestled just over
a hill from a beautiful blue lake. There was a long, long wooden
bridge that went from one side of the lake all the way over to the other
side of the lake. It was so far that no one could see the other end of the
long, long bridge.

The people of the village were very, very busy all the time. What did they do?
Why, all sorts of important things like delivering mail and building houses and
writing lots and lots of numbers to keep track of everything that was important.
They also ate lots of tasty foods like doughnuts and cupcakes and ice cream. They
especially loved ice cream. I think rum raisin was their favorite.

Every Sunday the people of the busy little village would meet in the town
square under the wide oak tree and talk about the beautiful blue lake just over the

hill from the town. Some would tell about men who had visited the lake many years before and brought back stories about how beautiful it really was. They told about how clear and deep the lake was and how laughing rainbow-colored catfish would swim right up to their boat, roll over, and ask them to pet their soft little bellies. They talked about how the ducks and turtles would sing a song to the sun while dogfish barked and wagged their tails in time to the music.

The people of the busy little village were happy when they talked about the lake on Sundays. But the next day, and all through the week, they forgot all about it and went back to the worries of being busy.

In the busy little village there lived a quietly happy girl named Sweet Little Martina. She had sunshine blond hair which flowed and jostled around her shoulders whenever she turned her head. Her deep brown eyes glistened like water in sunshine whenever they were open and probably did so when they were closed as well. Sweet Little Martina had tiny wooden crutches to help her walk because her legs were very, very weak. But she didn't seem to notice much for she would play with the other children of the busy little village from sun up to sun down. She never complained or said that it wasn't fair that she could not run or jump like the other children. Sweet Little Martina always greeted everybody with a big smile and happiness in her voice.

One reason that Sweet Little Martina was so happy was because her father and mother had taught her how to be brave and after that she was hardly ever afraid. And when she was afraid of a really, really bad storm with scary flashes of lightening and loud thunder, or if she thought that a monster might be living under her bed, she would remember what her mother and father had taught her and the scary parts would all go away. It even made the hurt in her legs go away. And if she fell over her crutches and scraped her hands and knees, as she would sometimes do when playing with the other children, she would do what her father and mother had taught her and the pain would stop. Her mother and father called it Quantum Entrainment (QE), but Sweet Little Martina liked to think of it as her happy place. She loved going to her happy place and would even go there when her legs weren't hurting or when she wasn't afraid. Her happy place was the reason why people said she had sunrise eyes.

Every morning Sweet Little Martina would sit in front of her mirror and brush her hair 100 times while she sang this hair brushing song:

Diddly-doo Diddly-dee
Won't you please look at me?
I'm a big girl, as you can see.
I brush my hair down to my knee.
Diddly-doo Diddly-dee
Diddly, diddly, diddly-dee.

Sweet Little Martina was very polite and very, very inquisitive. She loved to ask questions. Sometimes she would ask, "Where do clouds come from?" or "What is at the end of all the numbers?" or "Why can't I fly like the birds do?" If she could, she would fly high up in the sky with her arms stretched way out and when she got tired, she would lie down on a fluffy white cloud and look down on the people of the busy little village as they scampered around like wee little ants on a sugar cube.

One Sunday while her elders were telling stories about the beautiful blue lake, Sweet Little Martina tugged at the sleeve of the eldest elder and asked in her wee little voice, "Please excuse me, kind sir, but why don't we pack a picnic basket full of doughnuts and cake with bottles of cherry root beer, that tickles your nose when you drink it, and have a picnic by the side of the beautiful blue lake?"

A hush fell on all the town's people and they looked very serious indeed and the eldest elder said, "We can never go to the beautiful blue lake for under the long, long bridge lives an evil ogre." They told Sweet Little Martina that they never spoke about the ogre because they didn't want to scare little children, but he was twice as tall as a man and as big around as the big oak tree in the village square that they were sitting under that very moment. His skin was purple with green spots and it was slimy and smelly and bumpy. He had jagged green teeth with strings of old spaghetti hanging down because he never brushed after meals. He was a really naughty ogre. His breath smelled like tuna fish and broccoli and dirty socks all mixed together. The ogre had one red eye and one black eye and could see where he had been without turning around. That's why you could never sneak up from behind to catch him. Many brave men had tried and no one knows where they are now. His name was Ego the Ogre.

That night her daddy had read her a bedtime story about the good old days on the beautiful blue lake before Ego the Ogre came to live under the bridge. Sweet Little Martina wanted it to be that way again so that all the people of the busy little village could go on a wonderful picnic by the side of the beautiful blue lake. So as soon as the rooster crowed and the sun peeked its bright eye over the Long-way-away Mountains, she slipped out of bed, quiet as a mouse and put on her fuzzy slippers and outside clothes. Then she slipped into her wooden braces and started out for the long, long bridge over the beautiful blue lake on the other side of the hill at the edge of town.

On her way she listened to the birds singing to their babies in the nest:

Get up, get up you sleepy heads.
Shake your little tail feathers and open your beaks.
It's time for your wiggly breakfast worms
With marmalade and day-old leeks.

She giggled at the laughter of the leaves in the trees that were tickled by the quick morning breeze as it brushed against their bellies. By the side of the field where the old badger lived, she bent over and picked a single sunshine daisy, then she shambled down the dirt road all the way to the long, long bridge.

When she got to the long, long bridge, Sweet Little Martina stopped and listened and looked just like you do before crossing a street where cars go by. Everything was quite peaceful. She thought that maybe Ego the Ogre had met a lady ogre and had gotten married under the tall, tall bridge in the big busy city beyond the Long-way-away Mountains. She thought that maybe they moved under a respectable bridge in a good neighborhood where they could raise a family of two little ogres and own a pet rumplededumpleshnick, an ogre's best friend.

She shuffled slowly and quietly up to the end of the long, long bridge and waited. Nothing. Then she looked way across the long, long bridge but could not see the other side so she stepped forward. As soon as her tiny tippy-toe touched the first step on the bridge, she heard a deep rolling grumble like thunder coming from a dark basement. The bridge shook and swayed but the water beneath stayed calm and clear. Instead of running away, Sweet Little Martina (did I mention that she was a brave little girl?) said in her wee little voice, "Who's that under the bridge?"

The voice grew louder and grumpier and said, "It is I, Ego the Ogre. Do you want me to eat you up?"

"No," shivered Sweet Little Martina. "I only want to introduce myself and say hello."

"Go away before I have you with my breakfast of snakes and sawdust and, of course, my one-a-day multiple vitamin."

Sweet Little Martina was very afraid, but she went to her happy place and then she wasn't afraid anymore. She stood her ground and said in a pretend angry voice, "I will not leave until you come out and greet me like a proper gentleman."

The bridge shook more violently this time and Ego the Ogre's voice boomed and bounced off the Long-way-away Mountains into the faraway lands beyond the village. All the villagers heard the noise and came out of their houses in their nightgowns with cups of coffee sloshing on the ground, except the farmer who had been up for hours milking his cows. Everyone had nervous looks on their faces and worried tones in their voices. Then Sweet Little Martina's father and mother came running out of the house screaming, "Oh, where, oh, where can our Sweet Little Martina be? She's not in her bed and she has had no breakfast."

Then all of the town's people looked all over their village for Sweet Little Martina, but she was nowhere to be found. Then the eldest elder said, "I think she has gone to the long, long bridge across the beautiful blue lake over the hill at the edge of the village." The others agreed and they gathered all the weapons they could find. They got brooms and tennis rackets and willow branches and boxing gloves. One man even took the wobbly old sword from the statue of Horace the Ogre Slayer, which stood in the town square next to the wide oak tree.

While the town's folk were arming themselves and deciding who should be in the front of the line to rescue Sweet Little Martina, she was dealing with her own problems. As she stood with one toe on the bridge, Ego the Ogre was rising up from the mucky mud under the bridge to come and eat her. He crawled slowly out from under the long, long bridge with the mud sucking and slurping at his hands and knees. Then he shuffled and snuffled sideways as ogres always do, right up to the tiny little girl. Ego inflated himself like a great green goblin oozing purple slime. From his teeth, which looked like broken green glass, long strands of smelly old spaghetti dangled over his lips and down his chin just inches from her tiny little up-turned face.

He bellowed, "I'm going to eat you up."

Sweet Little Martina started to get afraid again as she looked up at that scary old ogre, but she was already in her happy place so she was only afraid for the blink of an eye, then it was gone. She stood there with her hands behind her back and said nothing at all. She knew it was wise to wait for someone who is angry to stop yelling before speaking. But the angry old ogre roared even louder, "Run away now or I will eat you this very moment."

Then in her teeny-tiny voice, Sweet Little Martina asked a question that stopped Ego the Ogre in his tracks. She asked, "Why?"

"Why?" he growled, his awful bad breath wrinkling Sweet Little Martina's nose. "Why? What do you mean why?"

"Why do you want to eat me?" she asked quietly.

"Because, because, uh. I want to eat you because..." But he couldn't finish the sentence. His mind just couldn't think of an answer. In fact, his mind couldn't think at all. This was most unusual, for Ego the Ogre always had thoughts. He had thoughts about eating little girls. He had thoughts about throwing mud on clean white sheets and stomping on butterflies and eating with his mouth open. He had all kinds of thoughts, but now his mind was completely still. And you know what? It felt good to stop thinking.

Ego the Ogre stuttered a little flustered, "I, uh...I can't think of it right now but I know I have a good reason tucked away in my memory somewhere. I...I just know I do."

But he didn't feel quite so confident now as he did a few moments ago.

Then Sweet Little Martina asked him something that made him go all jell-o like inside.

She asked in her teeny-tiny voice, "What do you want most of all?"

It was a simple enough question but somehow no matter how Ego the Ogre tried to answer the question, it didn't seem quite right. Did he want a treasure fit for a king? No. Did he want to eat Sweet Little Martina? Not really. He kinda liked this pale little human girl. Did he want more food, a clean new bridge to live under, or even a red toy fire engine that could go really, really fast? No, no, no! When he thought about it, he really didn't know what he wanted most of all. Maybe he wanted nothing.

Ego the Ogre looked down upon Sweet Little Martina's soft, innocent face and he felt confused because he really didn't want to hurt anyone or anything. As he looked at her, Sweet Little Martina brought her hands from behind her back and handed Ego the Ogre the single sunshine daisy that she had picked from the meadow by the side of the road. A giant green glistening tear formed in the ogre's black eye, rolled off his pointed cheek, and fell to the ground, making a crater in the dust.

Sweet Little Martina said, "Don't cry, Mr. Ogre. I will teach you how to find the happy place inside you and you will never be sad again."

And she did.

He felt his heart getting bigger and bigger like a balloon filled with helium gas. It felt like it was going to fill his whole chest so that he could float all the way up to Heaven. He was really, really happy for the first time in his life and he was very thankful to Sweet Little Martina for leading him to his happy place.

Then he bowed deep and swept his huge green arm toward the long, long bridge. And then he spoke in a gentle voice that made Sweet Little Martina feel even happier than before.

He said softly, "You may pass."

And she did.

Meanwhile, the town's people were moving slowly along the road to the long, long bridge to save Sweet Little Martina from the evil old ogre. They didn't know that she was already on her way over the long, long bridge to the other side of the beautiful blue lake. They were moving slowly because the ones in the front of the line kept finding excuses to go to the back of the line. Twenty-three town's folk had to stop and tie their shoes while the rest of the villagers walked past. Fourteen got rocks in their shoes or complained of blisters and had to sit down, and seven had sudden attacks of lumbago. Eleven just remembered that they left the burners burning on their stoves back in the busy little village. Most of them were men who never cooked a day in their lives but promised themselves that they would start cooking this very day as long as they did not have to come face-to-face with mean old Ego the Ogre.

Finally, the villagers arrived at the long, long bridge over the beautiful blue lake. They saw Ego the Ogre standing at the entrance of the long, long bridge smelling a daisy. They knew right away that it must be Sweet Little Martina's daisy because no self-respecting ogre would hold, much less smell, a dainty daisy.

The town's folk were very upset and very afraid and one yelled, "What have you done with our Sweet Little Martina?"

Ego the Ogre answered, "I let her go over the long, long bridge."

"Liar!" yelled one villager, "You have eaten her." And all the others joined in yelling and screaming and shaking their brooms and tennis rackets at the surprised ogre.

"It's true," he said, "She went over to the other side of the beautiful blue lake."

The villagers became more angry than they were afraid and pressed in toward Ego the Ogre. The man with the wobbly old sword stayed right behind the people in front. He thought that while Ego the Ogre was busy eating the people in front, he would have time to run away. Even though he had the wobbly old sword, he wasn't very brave. He only wanted people to think that he was brave.

Just then Ego the Ogre stepped forward to show the town's people the daisy and tell them that Sweet Little Martina gave it to him and she showed him where his happy place was and that she was now his friend. He wanted to tell them how she had cleared his mind of bad, bad thoughts and how he felt a funny feeling inside that made him happy and want to help instead of hurt. When he stepped toward them to show them the daisy, the people in the front of the line fell backward and the people behind the man with the wobbly old sword pushed him forward at the same time. The man with the wobbly old sword stumbled and fell forward and the sword stabbed Ego the Ogre in the left kneecap.

Now, if you or I were stabbed in the kneecap with a wobbly old sword, it might hurt a lot but we would be just fine after a little clean water and a bandage. But this is not so for ogres. The left kneecap is the only place that you can hurt an ogre. And a stab from a wobbly old sword is the only thing that can kill an ogre.

As the villagers watched, they saw Ego the Ogre fall down holding his knee and then a very strange thing happened. Ego the Ogre's body started to get lighter and lighter like it was turning into angel dust. Presently, it turned into light and then disappeared into thin air. One moment it was there and the next—poof—it was gone.

When he got stabbed in the left kneecap, Ego the Ogre felt a strange sensation like his heart really was expanding and he really did begin to float up to Heaven. On his way to Heaven, Ego the Ogre was looking down and saw the man who had stabbed him step forward and raise his wobbly old sword in the air yelling, "I did it! I killed the mean old ogre with my skill and cunning. I am the bravest man in the village and you should all buy me stuff and be nice to me forever and ever."

Right then another strange thing happened, but the villagers were getting used to strange things happening by now because this had been a day full of strange events and it wasn't even lunch time. What they saw happening to the man with the sword made them step back and say, "Oh."

The man with the wobbly old sword who was bragging about bravely killing the mean old ogre was changing. His skin was growing purple with green spots and it was becoming slimy and smelly and bumpy. He grew jagged teeth like broken green glass with strings of old spaghetti hanging down. His breath began to smell like tuna fish and broccoli and dirty socks all mixed together. And his eyes changed color: one red and one black. The town's folk began pointing and chanting, "Ego the Ogre, Ego the Ogre, Ego the Ogre."

The wobbly old sword fell from the man's hand, slid down the bank into the clear deep water of the beautiful blue lake, and was never seen again. And the bragging man really did turn into a mean old ogre. He was so ashamed, he slinked down the bank to hide under the long, long bridge. Later that night he stole away to live in a cave deep in the Long-way-away Mountains and was never seen again.

Then another strange thing happened. OK, OK, this is the last strange thing for this story, I promise. There, walking back from the other side of the beautiful blue lake was Sweet Little Martina smiling more sweetly than she had ever done before. And guess what? She was walking without crutches! All the villagers ran around her and lifted her up on their shoulders and her father and mother hugged and kissed her and told her how happy they were that she was alive.

They asked, "Where have you been?"

And Sweet Little Martina answered, "You know, I will tell you."

And this is what she told the villagers about her journey across the long, long bridge.

I walked a long, long way and I didn't think I would be able to walk all the way to the end of the long, long bridge on my crutches. I stopped to look into the water of the beautiful blue lake and I could see shimmering fishes singing and playing among the blossoming lake flowers down below. It was all very beautiful and I wanted to stay, but a little voice in my heart urged me to go on. So I did. I walked and I walked and I walked some more and then I finally saw the end of the long, long bridge. When I got to the end, I looked out over the land and there was nothing there. I peered into the nothingness for some time but still could not see anything. Then I stepped off the long, long bridge into the land of Nothing and I felt my feet get all tingly and begin to dissolve. It wasn't a bad feeling. It was wonderful—like stepping into a warm bath but without getting wet. Then my legs dissolved into nothing and my tummy and chest and arms and then my head all dissolved into nothing.

I don't know how long I was there, but I didn't fall asleep. I was awake but I didn't see or hear or feel anything. All of a sudden, I found myself standing back on the long, long bridge facing home. My crutches were lying on the bridge by my feet but I didn't need them anymore so I left them behind. I started walking the long way back home and then something remarkable happened. My feet floated off the long, long bridge up into the air. Up, up, up I went like a beautiful bird. I was flying! I flew over the clear waters of the beautiful blue lake but all I could see was a reflection of my Self looking back at me. It was so wonderfully wonderful. I felt brave and bright and very, very happy and it was like I loved everything. It was like my happy place had grown and grown to fill the whole wide world all at once.

I flew high up to the clouds and I didn't even get tired. I bounced from one cloud to another like trampolines with my hair almost bouncing off my head. It was so much fun. Then I lay on my back on a big billowy white cloud and looked straight up into Heaven. And you know what? I saw the most beautiful angel floating by. He had wide feathery wings of light and strands dangling from his teeth that looked a lot like strings of spaghetti made of angel light. He waved and blew me a kiss as he floated up and out of sight.

Then I rolled over on my tummy and peeked over the edge of the cloud and you know what I saw? I saw the beautiful blue lake with the long, long bridge going all the way over to the land of Nothing. Most of all, I saw all of you standing by the long, long bridge and you were all so very sad. So I flew down to see what was the matter. But now I am here. I see you are all very happy and that makes me happy, too.

The whole village started home again. Sweet Little Martina held her parent's hands as she walked. She looked lovingly up at her mother and then her father and when she saw them both at the same time, a deep unending love rose up in her heart. Her love engulfed her parents and when it spread to all the people of the busy little village, they became happy without needing to be so very busy. Sweet Little Martina walked with her mother and father and all the villagers back to the peaceful little village and they all lived happily ever after.

Back by the beautiful blue lake next to the long, long bridge at the very spot where Ego the Ogre's tear fell in the dust, there grew a single sunshine daisy.

The End

Teaching Your Child QE

The mind of a child naturally moves toward awareness of Eufeeling. This becomes less evident as a child grows. This is because of the influence of their control-oriented parents, teachers, and even their peers. As a child grows she forsakes the complete helplessness and freedom of infancy for the ability to manage and organize more and more the things and people in her environment. She must learn to live within imposed boundaries. This growth is necessary and good. We must learn to be self-sufficient if we are ever going to be Self-sufficient. We must give in to the pressures of adulthood. That is not the problem. The problem is that once we have learned how to control our lives, we must go on to reclaim the lost joys of childhood—the natural awareness of Self.

A child left on his own will perish. He must learn to survive. Once those skills have been mastered, that child becomes an adult. To complete the cycle of life, that adult must then revisit the magical realm of childhood and become reacquainted with his Self. There, the two halves become whole. The inner child has grown up and the adult becomes more childlike. The sum total is freedom expressed within boundaries, which is the best of both worlds. In essence, we can have our cake and eat it, too.

Out of ignorance or sloth, most adults do not return. This is the second most grievous crime an adult can commit. The first is to keep a child in ignorance of her Self. All the ills of humankind—and I mean *all* our ills—would vanish in a generation if our children could only learn to become free adults fully aware of their Self: that most refined level of creation, the home of Eufeeling. I am offering you that choice. Teach your child—teach every child—the simple rules of Self-awareness. Give her a chance to become free now and the choice of maintaining that freedom into adulthood. Let her learn that her Self is permanence permeating all change. Give her the greatest gift she could ever receive, then stand back and watch as peace quietly descends on Earth.

The ages at which a child can learn QE will vary depending on the child. You can start preparing your little one to learn QE as soon as he can identify feelings. If your child is very young, you may need to help him learn to identify positive and negative feelings before learning QE. This is especially valuable for the male child whose culture may encourage him to repress his emotions in preparation for manhood. Once a child knows what he is feeling, he can learn QE.

Kids' QE

- Do an activity that elicits a positive reaction in your child like happiness, fun, excitement, love, etc.

  The quieter the emotion, the easier to look inward, so happiness and love would be preferable to excitement or fun. Reading a book like *Sweet Little Martina and the Mean Old Ogre* where the characters express feelings is an excellent quiet activity for our purposes.

- Once your child is feeling a positive emotion, ask him or her to identify that emotion.

- Then ask him to be very quiet and look at or feel that emotion to see what happens. Do this for only 5 or 10 seconds as the child's mind will want to wander to other things.

- Point out that when he quietly watches his feeling, he begins to feel quieter or happier inside.

  "When you quietly watch your good feeling, see how it makes you feel happy inside?"

- Ask him to watch the happiness, or whatever Eufeeling he is having, and tell you what happens. He may then tell you what he is thinking or sensing or tell you a story.

- Let him talk for a minute or so, then have him pause and ask him if his good feelings are still there. He will say, "yes."

- Ask him to again watch his good feeling and point out how it makes him feel happy inside.

- Continue with this cycle even after the activity has ended. In a short time, you will only have to remind your child to look inward for their happy feeling and they will have it immediately. Soon your child will come to realize that their good feeling (Eufeeling) is always there. This joy they will carry into adulthood and share with the rest of our Eufeeling-starved world.

The Beginning...

APPENDIX A
Frequently Asked Questions and Answers

Contents

1. Can QE help me love myself?

I ride to work on a bicycle every morning. It's a very nice trip about 10km through a lovely wood. When I'm there, I'm in touch with a lot of energy. Yesterday I spontaneously had these good feelings and so I said to myself that it should be possible for me to breathe deeper and stronger now. I just QE'ed in my mind and a few moments later my breathing felt very much stronger. I thanked the universe for this experience.

I have two questions. For a few months, I have had feelings of depression about not being able to love myself. My parents taught me that it's important to do your best for others but not for myself. Is it possible that I can heal myself with QE? If so, how? This problem holds much emotion for me and I do not have the right energy for doing QE.

The second question is easy. Am I allowed to do QE for people without their knowing about it? Or, do I have to ask their permission? I feel QE will help us save ourselves and our Earth.

Answer: Thank you for your kind words. The world, like you and I, is pure awareness. On one level, there is no need to save anyone or any thing. It is the perception of differences that allows ego to separate and categorize into negative and positive. It will all work out in the end. Our best bet is to do QE and increase our awareness of pure awareness. Really, that is all we can, or need to do. The rest will take care of itself. You will see.

Now, let's address the problem of loving yourself. There are two selves: the little self, or me, and the universal Self that is undying, pure Love. The little self I like to refer to as "me" to eliminate confusion. "Me" is the relative, changeable part of us that has a past and future. It doesn't have a present. The present is where the Self lives. "Me" is what you think you are. You might say you are a woman, 35 years old, a mother, who doesn't like your work but who loves to walk in the woods. Do you see? The "me" is restricted and changeable. The Self is not. The Self is the first glimmering of awareness in form. Do you know what another name for the Self is? The Self is also known as Eufeeling.

That's right. The Self is Eufeeling. So, Self love is simply awareness of the Eufeeling. Isn't that true? When you are aware of Eufeeling, you feel good, don't you? You feel quiet or peace or joy or bliss. First, become aware of pure awareness and then pay attention to the feeling you get; that is your Eufeeling or your inner and infinite Self. You will always accept your Self when you are aware of it. It is just that easy. QE is a direct method of Self love. Just keep doing QE in all its forms and you will fall more and more deeply in love with your Self.

You do not need the permission of anyone when you do QE. That is because you are not doing anything. You just have your own intention and then become aware of pure awareness and let pure awareness do all the work. In reality, there is no you or me or them. There is only one awareness and one does not need permission to do anything to Itself. Actually, one can't do anything but we'll save that story for another time. Me and you and all this stuff of the apparent universe is only an illusion; it is a dream of separateness. Pure awareness and Eufeeling allow us to wake and watch the dream unfold. It is like when we are asleep and start dreaming and are aware that we are dreaming (lucid dreaming). Only we become aware that we are dreaming the waking dream. We dip into pure awareness, which cleanses any negative or wrong intentions. We can do no harm with QE so if we are not supposed to QE someone else, it will not work. It is just that simple.

2. Can QE help emotional problems?

My partner suffers from emotional problems. Can QE help?

Answer: We don't have to worry about why someone is suffering, for instance, from a bad childhood or self-esteem problems. We don't even have to know what caused a physical complaint like back pain or a sprained ankle. We only have to know pure awareness. Once we become aware of pure awareness, healing takes place all by itself, for both our partner and ourselves. Pretty neat, huh?

You see, when we turn our awareness away from pure awareness, then we forget that it is the harmonizing power of all things created. We get swept away by the waves of our everyday lives. When we anchor to the ocean of pure awareness, then the waves of worry and woe cannot wash us off course. Well, I guess I've pushed this analogy a little too far, but you see what I mean. Your partner is overwhelmed by the results of his actions missing the deeper meaning...absolute peace.

QE does not heal anything. People and techniques don't heal. Awareness of pure awareness heals. QE shows us how to be aware of pure awareness. If your partner becomes aware of pure awareness, then he will heal. He will heal by the wisdom of pure awareness and not our timetable. So be prepared to do QE and then just watch to see what happens. For this reason, I can't tell you how many QE sessions it will take. I can only tell you that all problems eventually yield to the ultimate healing power of pure awareness. And they do that faster and more fully in every way.

3.   Can QE effect the weather?

We have very strong weather—hot and thundery—and I find it very stressful for my emotions and my body. Will QE help?

Answer: Rig Veda pundits can effect the weather. A friend of mine told me how he watched them make clouds appear and disappear right overhead. If they can do it, why not you? I once did the same thing but then got so excited and full of myself that I could never duplicate the feat. Here's how to go about effecting the weather. Briefly think your intention and then do QE. If you find yourself sitting in a puddle of your own sweat and swatting mosquitoes, then do QE again. Sooner or later, the weather will change. It always does. You can take credit for it if you want, but better you just do QE and then count the rivulets of sweat running down your face.

The weather and other environmental factors will always have an influence on your body/mind. Even in the midst of all your emotional discomfort is peace. Look for the stillness and in that stillness, you will find peace; it may be sweaty peace, but better sweating and at peace than sweating and angry or fearful.

4.   Do I really have to touch the partner?

I am a psychotherapist in Germany and have a question for you. Is it really necessary to touch the client? Doesn't it have an effect if I am just in awareness during while the client tells me the problem? Shouldn't awareness find the right solution and show the next step for the client? I work with my normal methods, but I trust in another power that leads the process.

Shouldn't pure awareness accompany us all the time and be able to heal other people without knowing anything about it? A big problem and danger is, in my opinion, that our ego immediately wants to claim successes as a personal achievement. The ego says, "I am a big healer now!" I think somebody must be very mature to work with that method. Do you think that the ego also could grow with the QE-Method?

Answer: No, it is not necessary to touch the partner. (See the chapter on Remote QE in *The Secret of Instant Healing*.) When you do QE, there is really no "other" power. There is only pure awareness. In reality, there is nowhere to go and nothing to do. But it appears that healing needs to be accomplished and that we start the process and then watch as it unfolds. I have to teach this way to build a bridge from common thinking to no-thinking.

Do not mix Quantum Entrainment (QE) with other concepts, ideas, feelings, sensations, or anything else. QE is most effective as it is. If you want to add another technique, do it after QE. Using ideas or feelings brings you back out into the mind—the playground of ego. When you do QE exactly as taught, ego will let go, not get stronger. With time, QE will eventually allow ego to play and have fun in the field of relativity but not take control. The ego becomes more like a pet dog that is lovable, mischievous, and loves to play. This is a joyful state of being and not beyond the grasp of the person who does QE often throughout the day.

5. Do I have to know the reason for the problem?

I have been practicing applied kinesiology under Dr. Klinghardt. Every emotional problem or every disease cannot exist without a reason. Now, if you are healing someone with QE, the reason for this problem already exists—and so I think the problem may return if the person doesn't change the reason it is there. Am I right?

Answer: As for emotional problems...well, any problems, it doesn't matter what the cause. The solution is more pure awareness. Traditional thinking is cause and effect. And, if you find and remove the cause; you can eliminate the effect. This works on the relative level of life, but we have found a more fundamental way to approach the problem of problems. We let Eufeeling do the healing. We don't have to change our ways... Eufeeling changes them for us. You can, and should, continue to do your relative healing techniques. Just add QE to the beginning and Eufeeling will guide the results. Those physicians who take this approach find that their practices are improved. They don't work as hard and the results are deeper and more far reaching.

It has been my clinical experience that the changes are remarkably stable. But of course we need more research to firmly make this statement. My suggestion is to do QE and observe the results. The more pure awareness one realizes, the more harmony one appears to radiate. Let me know what your investigations turn up.

6. How many QE teachers are there in the world?

My sister told me about a man who is teaching QE here in Germany. She said he was trained by you to teach QE. I was not sure about this. Can you tell me how many teachers for QE are in the world?

Answer: At present, there is only one QE teacher in the world and guess who that might be...Right! That would be me. While the QE rapid healing process is easy to learn, one must not only be clearly and deeply aware of pure awareness but they must also understand how it apparently manifests in all levels of our lives. I doubt that a person who is teaching a technique and calling it QE is really expressing the deeper values of the QE process or experiencing pure awareness clearly. If they were, then they would develop their own technique instead of borrowing from another. When we are fully aware of pure awareness, there are no limitations. There is enough to go around for everybody.

I wrote this book so that anyone who wanted to could learn to do QE by themselves. That is what I want, above all else—to see millions of people becoming aware of pure awareness and the best and quickest way I know to do that is through QE. Awareness of pure awareness is the birthright of every human being and because it is, it is natural and easy to learn. I know of many people who have learned QE from reading this book and taught others to do it. That makes me feel very good indeed. Teaching QE one-on-one is a wonderful human bonding experience on the deepest level. Of course, there will be impurities and inaccuracies passed along with the teaching; that is expected. But these impurities will all dissolve in time because the very process of becoming aware of pure awareness will fix them. In my experience, others who have tried to teach QE to groups have created more harm than good. A group exponentially increases the transmission of error, and a single mistake on the teacher's part will be amplified manifold.

Be patient. As more people practice QE, there will be more people aware of pure awareness. Then I will make teachers and then we can be sure that it will be awareness of pure awareness that increases exponentially.

7. What intention should I use for chronic diseases like ALS?

I am 30 years old and I am diagnosed with amyotrophic lateral scle-

rosis (ALS). That's the same disease Stephen Hawking is suffering from. Mainstream medicine does not have any idea how to stop or influence its progress so I am searching for alternative ways to fight against this disease. Because I am also a fan of the modern philosophy of quantum physics, I bought your book three days ago and I can say, I love it! Your method seems to be very powerful, but I have some problems feeling the pure awareness outside my body when I follow your exercise. I practice every day.

Is it possible to use your technique for self-healing? How should I formulate this intention for healing? This disease is very complex and you said that the intention should be precise and simple.

Answer: Yes, you can self-heal with QE but in the beginning it is usually easier to heal others than yourself because you tend to be very attached to your personal healing needs and that will just get in the way.

While QE is not an energy technique, when you become aware of pure awareness, healing energy is created and naturally goes where it is needed. With ALS, as with any chronic disease or condition, your body/mind will absorb a great deal of healing energy and you may not see results right away, but they will come. What results and to what degree is unknown. Miraculous things happen when you become aware of pure awareness. While you should be optimistic, you should also be realistic. In all likelihood, your disease will continue to progress. If you are not cured with QE, then you will most definitely be helped physically, mentally, and emotionally. The real value is in losing your attachment to the body/mind and finding inner peace. Even while your physical condition may decay, awareness of your inner essence will free you from suffering and release you from the confines of this disease.

Your intention to heal should be very gentle and you should

not attach to it at all. That is, just have a simple thought of what you would like to happen, do QE, and then let it go. "Let it go" means to go on with your life not looking for results. You'll notice them when they appear. When the results come and you are not looking for them, then you know they are real. That is how simple it all is. The less involved you are in the outcome, the more effective it will be. Do QE and live; that's it.

8. Why does doing QE on your self seem less effective?

I read your book with great interest and immediately began to do the exercises. After several attempts on myself, I had very few results. However, I did feel particularly happy one day. I am not sure whether I am doing this method correctly. Is it better to practice on somebody else first? Could it be that I must develop awareness beforehand? I have had experience with meditation, Reiki, EFT, etc., which I thought may be of some benefit. My main problem is bronchial / nasal and I often have to cough. I'm probably also allergic. I would most appreciate hearing from you for a short guideline as I am going on a two-week holiday to a North Sea island this Saturday where I plan to practice— or, rather, try to heal myself.

Answer: It is sometimes better to start working on someone else. When you work on yourself, you keep watching, looking for results and lose awareness of pure awareness. Frequently review the instructions on how to do QE in Section I until you feel comfortable with doing QE. It should be easy, effortless, and fun. Don't make it a chore. Eufeeling is subtle. You can't bully your way through the process. It's not like building a bird house where you get all the pieces and then force them together with nails and glue. QE is a gentle dismantling process, much like watching a sand castle dissolve back into the sea.

A wonderful thing you can do is go to the QE website (www. QuantumEntrainment.com) and sit in on the QE Forum. There, people from all over the world come together in the spirit of sharing what they have learned about QE and helping others understand the practical applications of QE. There is even a thread for people who would like to receive or give QE remotely. The QE Forum is lively, supportive, and inspiring.

Another suggestion is to find a friend or someone who wants to practice QE with you and work with each other. Do it every day, many times if it is possible; the more, the better. You don't even have to get together physically because QE works just as well remotely. The more you give the more you will heal. This is a very important and powerful healing principle. Give, give, give with no concern for getting and you will be amazed at the results.

By far, the best thing you can do is to practice QE on yourself and on other people as often as you can; 20 or 30 times a day is ideal. Do remote and extended sessions multiple times daily. With chronic conditions like yours, it just takes time. Of course, you would also seek the proper treatment from a physician. First do these things and then let me know how you are doing. I will help you where I can. Taking the QE Workshops are enormously helpful.

9. Is QE less effective when I do it for family?

I'm urgently looking for help for my husband. He's mentally and physically ill and he is also afraid of so many things and people. He has not been out of the house for many years. He cannot sleep at night and he has, among other things, dyspnea, diabetes, abdominal pain, and other pain. My greatest fear is that he could die.

I'm not able to support or help him because I feel helpless, small, and guilty about his situation. For this reason, I see a psychologist. I am reading your fantastic book and I have hope that QE will be able to help us both.

Answer: If you know someone else who does QE, have them work on him even if it is remotely. I think you might be too close to the problem and since you are new to QE you are probably looking for results, which is the best way *not* to get them. This is natural when you first start QE as you desperately want to see changes. QE works best when you go to pure awareness and then let it do the healing. You may not see results for some time and then all of a sudden, a miracle happens.

With the intensity of your husband's problems, you might not see much of a change initially. It is best for you and someone else to work with him. I don't know what his mental capacity is or where his inclinations lie, but if at all possible, have him learn to do QE and have him do it for others. That will be good for him. It will help him heal much more than working on himself.

10. How does QE Compare to Matrix Energetics?

I am a medical doctor and if this is not too big of a request, I would be very pleased if you could give me a brief note about the advantage of your method in comparison to matrix energetics from Richard Bartlett.

Answer: This is a very good question and a comparison between the two techniques would be interesting if not valuable. Unfortunately, I am not qualified to make that comparison. I have only read Dr. Bartlett's book and I found it informative and inspiring. I have had many Matrix practitioners in my workshops, but all in all, I could not comment on either the philosophy or the practice of Matrix Energetics with any authority.

I am an expert on QE, however, and what I can do is give you a little deeper understanding of the mechanics of QE and let you draw your own conclusions.

QE is advaita, the philosophy espoused by Eckhart Tolle and Ramana Maharishi, made manifest. The QE process establishes the practitioner in the non-moving Now and, while bathing in this all-pervasive pure awareness, observes while healing takes place without effort of any kind. It's a kind of lazy person's path to inner enrichment and Self-awareness.

During a QE session, the partner will first start to feel relaxed in the body because of the deep rest that accompanies the QE process. Then peace will dawn in the mind and heart. This experience will quickly deepen and the body may begin to sway or bend as each cell is infused with awareness of pure awareness. At this point, the mind may experience long periods free of thought. This is also the time when bliss or joy can manifest and all seems right with the world, and it is. The results are many times dramatic and even miraculous—especially to the non-QE mind. To QEers, it's business as usual.

The person receiving QE may also bend or sway and occasionally swoon as a deep sense of relaxation and bliss washes over them. Following the philosophy that simpler is more powerful, QE looks to remove and refine toward the simplest and most powerful state of pure awareness. Healing is actually a side effect of becoming aware of pure awareness.

QE really isn't a healing technique but rather a process for deep inner work quickly leading to profound inner awareness. It's pretty remarkable when you think of it. You simply become aware of your inner Self and healing takes place without you doing anything. QE emphasizes the stillness beyond the mind. The QE practitioner finds and holds pure awareness and watches to see how it reflects in the mind. The emphasis is on non-doing and the results are profoundly different.

Encouraging the mind is to encourage the infinite differences of life. This is how we normally see our world moving—from relationship to relationship, job to job, etc. It is the rocky road of fleeting happiness, struggle, and confusion. When the mind is anchored in non-changing, unbounded pure awareness, the road smooths out and peace and harmony begin to dominate.

QE is neither an outward-oriented energy healing system nor an inner-oriented silent meditation technique. QE is a combination of both and therein lays its genius. QE anchors the mind in pure awareness while it is enthusiastically performing activity, giving it the best of both worlds and quickly opening one's consciousness to the inner Self and the peace that comes with it.

The QE practitioner does not create vibrations or manipulate matter, nor does she sit silently searching for enlightenment. When healing, eating, or loving, she simply becomes aware of pure awareness and then watches while life unfolds in that all-permeating pure awareness. Because QE is a natural process of human consciousness, it is easily and quickly learned even from a book. Breathing is a natural expression of every human being. You don't have to learn how to breathe; all you need is air. Likewise, you don't have to learn how to heal. All you need is pure awareness.

11. What can I do to be aware?

I have not slept a second all week. Yesterday I visited the doctor and I got medication. My problems are also connected with my work where I am experiencing stress. I get too little time for all household tasks and this leads my body and soul into a ruin. I get constant fast heartbeat and I cannot relax at night or fall asleep. In addition, there are fears about the future. I cannot switch my thinking and that draws nothing good to me. Unfortunately, I have nobody around me who could help me with the QE. I live my life alone. The only thing that is available for me is the Internet. When I cared for my departed son, I lost many friends and acquaintances. My life spins in a circle from which I gladly would like to escape, but I cannot help myself.

Although I have read your book, I did not manage to practice the QE. My third eye (or pure awareness) is not opened. I really don't know how to continue.

Answer: Your desire to be free will eventually find its way to fruition. You do not have to open your third eye to be aware. You are already aware; otherwise, you would not be aware that you needed to open your third eye. See what I mean? You don't need to do anything but be aware that you are aware and let the rest take care of itself. It probably will take time but not necessarily. Out of the greatest difficulties comes the greatest salvation. Ramana Maharishi and Tolle both thought they were dying. My shift came after some years of turmoil as I think did Karl Renz's. Anyway, be aware of your discomfort. Don't try to evade it or hide from it. You have attached a good deal of emotion to your situation. Do you know how I define a problem? A problem is a situation that you attach negative emotion to. So a walk in the rain could be a situation or a problem, depending on whether you join it with a negative emotion. Look at your problems, emotions, and thoughts without judging. If you do judge, watch your mind while it is judging. As you clearly and intently observe your problems, the pain will quickly leave. If it comes back, do it again. Soon the situation will remain but you will be free of the negative emotion that is causing your suffering.

12. Can QE make me tired and confused?

The last two or three days that I've been doing QE, my head is empty and I'm foggy and a little confused.

Answer:
There could be several reasons for your foggy thinking; lack of food, lack of rest, stress, etc. It could also be because of the QE, but that is very unlikely unless you did it for many hours. QE is very potent in releasing stress and healing the body. If you do QE for long periods, hours per day, you could have lazy or foggy thinking. This is due to your body/mind needing extra rest to heal. That will also make you sleepy because sleep and rest is what the body needs to complete the healing started on the very subtle and powerful level of the Eufeeling. Get your rest and it should dissolve in a day or two. If it doesn't, then look for another reason for your cloudy thinking and fatigue. You may need to consult a qualified health care physician.

13. Can I do too much QE?
Can I do QE with chronic conditions?

How often do you advise to give QE - what intervals?
In case of severe diseases, [should it be given] more often? or "only" extended QE?

Answer:
You can't do QE too much, but you can get a little disoriented,

especially with extended remotes. If that happens, then more physical activity and fresh air will quickly stabilize the results.

Chronic problems are invitations to do QE as much as possible. Chronic illness will soak up the effects of QE like a sponge. Do as much as you like. Even so, don't look for results.

Stay with your condition but also QE the lab tests, machines, etc. Again, do this without expectation. Do QE and go on with your life as before. That is how to get the best result, by eliminating fear and expectation. It is fear that keeps us stuck in the boundaries of the condition. During QE, your perception will become unbounded. If it is allowed to enter back into the same belief system, then you will reacquire the same condition. We are all confined by our perceptions so we need to do QE frequently, waiting for the time when we reemerge into complete freedom.

It is doubt and disappointment that keeps us locked into our condition. Don't try and remove doubt, just do QE and take what you get. That is the quickest way to liberation.

14. Can one QE session be deeper than another?

The second Remote QE session I did with you were incredibly deep and much healing took place almost instantly. Why was one deeper and more effective than the other?

Answer:

In pure awareness or with Eufeeling, there is no "deeper." It may feel deeper or different, but that is subjective and has nothing to do with the results. Whatever our subjective feeling, Eufeeling always does a complete job of healing. Your physical, emotional, or social concerns always get the full dose, for lack of a better way of saying it, even if we want more. We can never know completely what is best for any problem when considering all the possible causes and effects. Eufeeling does. Healing goes on every time, whether we recognize it or not. Or more accurately, pure awareness and Eufeeling is perfect and we either realize it or we don't. That, of course, is also perfect.

15. How do I use surrogates? Can I QE a whole group of people?

Concerning the use of substitutes (surrogates) in the QE long-distance healing, you write that it is possible to use a photograph or even just the name [of someone] on a piece of paper. In such a case, have we to place the fingers on the photo or on muscles of our own body? And is it possible to apply the healing on a whole group of persons? In the last case, how could we place the fingers somewhere? From the logical point of view, it should be possible, as the pure awareness includes all of them in it, but I am not sure about the practical application.

Answer:

The surrogate is simply a way to focus your mind. It is not necessary to be very specific. Eufeeling will know where to go and what to do. You just give Eufeeling a nudge in the direction you would like it to move, then step back and watch. You can use fingers or not; that's up to you. If you use your fingers, you can place them on your body, a picture, in the air, or anywhere you like.

As for QE-ing a group of people at one time, of course; why not? I often do a group at one time or have a group present in my imagination. Then I work with each person in the group individually while I hold the whole group in pure awareness. Pure awareness manifests through Eufeeling differently for each of us so I invite you to explore and experiment. QE is not written in stone. It is written in Nothing. Play and have fun. The more boundaries you break, the more you will be amazed.

16. How can QE improve finances and relationships?

I have read all three of your books. Now I know how to cure health and emotional problems using QE, but how do I manifest change in [other] areas in my life? For example, how do I improve my finances and relationships and so on? How would the QE process be applied to these areas—especially if I do not know what is best for me, because I do not know the big picture of my life? So, how important is the intent in this scenario?

For example, if I want to have a girlfriend, would the intent, "I am in a loving relationship with a wonderful woman," be OK?

Answer: The trick is to realize that you are not in control and so you cannot really do anything to make life turn out how you want. When we try satisfying a desire, on one side of the coin, we find false-fullness like happiness and pride—and, on the other side of the coin, disappointment, frustration, and suffering. The beauty of life is in its simplicity. Look for that. Oddly enough, when you simplify, your life only gets fuller. Yes, I know it sounds a bit cryptic, but there you have it. Life is full of seeming contradictions but actually life is completely harmonious as it is.

So, that's the first part; you must realize that you are not in control and that life is perfect as it is. Obviously, if life is perfect, then you don't need to be in control. Neat, huh? It is the ego that mucks everything up. It wants to make things happen in a way that makes it feel secure. Of course, it will never feel complete so taking the ego's way is the way of pieces. You get a piece of happiness, a piece of sadness, a piece of elation, and a piece of fear and anxiety. But, you can never get a piece of peace! First of all, you can't get what you already have and, secondly, you can't break peace into pieces.

What you are ultimately asking for is a piece of peace. "Give me money or a great relationship and I'll be satisfied and at peace." Why not go right to the source of peace—pure awareness? Well, that's what you've decided to do and that's a very good thing. But your mind is still looking at the pieces. You see, the fullness of peace has not worked its way into your thinking. It will soon as you continue to be aware of pure awareness by doing QE.

Now, you don't have to believe this or try to work it out logically. The heart and the mind are two different paths to enlightenment but both fail just before the realization of perfection is made. So, what to do? All this theory is well and fine but what about "me" stuck in the "real" world? What can I do? The answer is still the same: nothing. You can do nothing and as soon as you realize this simple truth, the goal of every thought, word, and action will be realized in its fullness.

You feel that your life is your own. That is, you have made the choices that have brought you to your present position. And you can make choices now, in the present, that will affect your life in the future. But you also know that now is all there is. It is your mind that keeps creating time as a way to work beyond your present condition. You feel a lack and that spurs you on to change. That makes sense, doesn't it? It makes sense to the mind but you are not your mind, right? You are awareness. You learned that in the first few pages of every one of my books. When you forget you are awareness, you fall softly back into the clutches of the time-oriented mind. So, how do you work out of it? Again, you go beyond working and succeed by doing nothing. And how do you do nothing? QE!

You already have the answer to your question theoretically, and I have been playing with you a little but for a good reason. If you rely on QE to get you "things," then you are playing in the field of the ever-changing mind. The value of QE is that you first "know" your Self and then let things come as they will. You see? QE gently invites you to let go of control and rewards you with all kinds of things when you do. But forget for just a moment and give more value to those things than your Self and you have turned QE into just another energy-healing technique. Don't forget your Self. Don't forget to be aware of pure awareness. Then you will find that all will come to you. In fact, more will come to you than you could think possible. That's the simple truth. Be aware and then let life come to you. That's it! No more is necessary.

Try this experiment the next time you drive a car. Instead of thinking you are in a car moving over the streets and through the city, see yourself as sitting stationary in the car and all the buildings, cars, and people are coming to you. Notice that you feel more relaxed, less stressed when things are coming to you. It is just a shift in perspective, but it makes a difference in how we feel and behave. So it is with realizing we are pure awareness. When we do, our world is created without our involvement. We become an innocent witness as creation unfolds before us. What a joy! We are simply aware. Nothing more is needed.

To answer your question specifically, simply become aware of what you want in the most innocent and general way and then do QE. You can do QE on your body, use a surrogate, or just use your imagination. Have that innocent idea of what you want and then let it go. Let pure awareness take it, nurture it, and then give it back to you more completely than you had imagined. Sit with your heart. That is, become aware of your Eufeeling and just be in that simple awareness of Self. You see? Soon you will give up the idea of wanting or needing and that is when you will get all that you really want.

17. Can the "Law of Attraction" cause more problems?

By using QE and the exercises (The Gate Technique & Pure Awareness Technique), I become more peaceful. Even if my body sometimes experienced fear reactions, like sweating, I am more and more at peace.

I have done what you have mentioned. I was feeling the desire and I was using QE on it, without using an intention statement, and I have to say, I felt very good in just a matter of minutes. I was feeling my desire to have a girlfriend, I visualized it, and used QE on it, and now I feel pretty good.

So, if I am working on a fear I have, wouldn't it be better to visualize the situation I am afraid of, then use QE, in contrast to just using a statement like "I am now free of...."

I also have to say I like your "philosophy" of not trying to control life. I mean, there are many "spiritual teachings" like the Law of attraction, which are basically putting you back in your mind, and making you crave material things even more. The opposite is true with QE. You let go of all desire and let Eufeeling do for you what is best.

Answer: You are right about the Law of Attraction philosophy creating greater desire. Thank you for your observation. This is a very vital point to ponder. Clear observation of what is will quell all desire by filling us with the goal of all desire, pure awareness. No need to try and manipulate things, thoughts, and ideas to get what you need. Be purely aware and you are home free.

And yes to your first observation. Bringing up the offending emotion or emotional event and then doing QE will be far more successful than a mere statement of intention. (Review Chapter 15, Psychological Healing, in *The Secret of Instant Healing*.)

18. What is the difference between pure awareness and Eufeeling? Why do we need a technique?"

The idea to apply the power of "pure awareness" is for me, as a theoretical physicist, of great importance, not only because it conforms with the results of my science, but also because it is free of any beliefs and any dogma! And of course because it gives to everybody the possibility for direct applications in the own life and for the life on our whole planet!

Now, I have a few questions about the application of QE.
1. On listening to your MP3 "pure awareness process," I could not feel anything at the end! I would not say that I had a "feeling" but rather a complete emptiness, just a "not feeling"! Is that OK or did I somehow process it wrong?

2. On applying QE for persons living far away or even for the whole environment, I am not quite sure how to do it.

3. Why do we need a technique? Is it not enough just to be in the pure awareness?

Answer: 1. The feeling of nothing is just right. Nothing is Bohm's Implicate Order or pure awareness; not to be confused with zero point or vacuum state. In the state of nothing, when you pay close attention, you will find that your body is relaxed and your mind is very peaceful. This peace is Eufeeling. The Eufeeling is akin to zero point and is the first glimmer of individual awareness. It is both unbounded and individual. That is, the universal aspect of the individual. I also refer to it as the Self. Your focus was on pure awareness, that is all. The Eufeeling was there with it, but your perspective was on nothing; pure awareness. Good for you.

2. Yes, for Remote QE you can use your own body, a picture, your imagination, a stuffed animal, whatever feels most natural to you. Be sure to *not* look for results. That is very important. Just do the Remote QE and take what comes. You'll be surprised.

3. Technique is a learning tool. It releases the mind from things and allows it to become infused with pure awareness/Eufeeling. If you can go right to pure awareness, then that is fine. This is pure QE, pure awareness without the pretense of trying. It is really the only way one can experience pure awareness. The QE technique just tricks the mind into not thinking.

19. Do I need the Pure Awareness technique to do QE?

How can one be in a state of pure awareness without going through the Pure Awareness technique? Can you explain please? (Get free download of the Pure Awareness Technique on the QE website.)

Answer: Actually, one cannot be out of the state of pure awareness. The question is, "Are we aware of pure awareness?" But, to answer your specific question, QE allows the mind to slip its attraction to forms of things and ideas and actually experience unboundedness. I offer the Pure Awareness technique to make awareness of pure awareness very obvious. Some people like the idea that it is guided and listen to it every day. But, you can do it just as easily and far more quickly by doing QE.

There are infinite ways to become aware of pure awareness. For instance, the Shiva Sutras list 112 ways to free the mind of boundaries. In order to teach one to quickly become aware of pure awareness, I developed QE which allows easy and immediate access to that ocean of nothing, which, when contacted, reflects peace and bliss in the mind.

20. Can QE help genetic diseases?

My teenage children love to listen to your Gate Technique. (Get free download of the Gate Technique on the QE website.) We do it together nearly every day. Young people today are so wonderfully open for what is right. They do not have intellectual resistance to accepting something new.

My blood pressure is too high, about 140:95. My doctors say it runs in the family and it is called hereditary hypertension and it can't be changed. I feel like a candle lit on both ends, which will burn out faster.

I applied QE the last two early mornings in bed when I woke up worrying about my momentary financial situation. Measuring my blood pressure before breakfast, it was below 90 yesterday and today. Is this a sign of small success? Would you have a tip on how I could tackle this not being able to relax deep inside? I think that you are absolutely right about the pure awareness healing all and everything.

Answer: You are right; QE will help blood pressure. QE has been known to have a marked effect on blood pressure when done regularly. In fact, so will the Gate Technique. (Get free download of the Gate Technique on the QE website.)There is new evidence that a genetic condition can be changed. We *do* *not* have to resign ourselves to being the slaves to our genes. Pick up a book called *Genie in the Genes* by Dawson Church or *The Biology of Belief* by Bruce Lipton. I think you will be encouraged. The latest research suggests that perception can alter gene function. When we do QE our perception slips the bonds of boundaries altogether. And you don't even have to believe in QE for it to work. Perception of pure awareness works on the whole body/mind at once. It offers your mind something it can get in no other way—total freedom. Your mind is always occupied with the stuff and things of everyday life and this creates mental friction, so to speak. This friction comes from one thought after another. This causes us to feel that there is no end to thoughts and things. They come so fast, we can't appreciate them and we may find ourselves asking, "Is this all there is to life?" The answer is, "No, there is more...or, actually, less." When it comes to balance and harmony in your mind, less is better but nothing is best. Pure awareness is the nothing that quiets your mind and soothes your body.

21. How can I do QE when I am attached to the results?

I already told you of my very sick dog Marcie. The problem has not changed yet. I gave her QE every day, but I could not succeed. You said that I may be too attached to Marcie. How can I help my dog without being attached? This dog is my child (I have no kids), and it hurts me so much to see her suffering. I know that I am like this, but it is not easy to not be attached.

Answer: You may be doing QE the right way. There is no way to know unless I was able to check how you are doing it. Don't worry over your technique. You can be attached to Marcie and that is just fine. Just don't be attached to the results of the QE. Do you understand the difference? Love your dog deeply but be very casual about QE. If you are doing QE properly, then whatever happens is just right. Eufeeling decides what gets healed and when, not you and I. That is the hardest part for many people to accept, but when they do, their lives change in a most miraculous way. When they do, they see all things and circumstances as perfect just as they are. That does not mean there isn't conflict. Conflict is seen on the local, limited level. Perfection is known when awareness of pure awareness dawns. Then even conflict is accepted as a vital and brilliant part of the whole.

Please don't worry about whether you are doing QE correctly. Just go back and read the instructions again. Then have fun with QE. Start on small stuff like aches and pains. Once you see success there, you are ready for the major and chronic problems that you face. You might also pick up a copy of my first book, *Beyond Happiness: How You Can Fulfill Your Deepest Desire*. Skip to the last chapter, "When You Become Enlightened." Reading it will help you understand some of the problems you face and ground you more completely in the workings behind the QE process.

22. Will QE help angry people?

Do you have experiences with QE treating very aggressive people? My nephew is very aggressive and tends to violence. His father has been this way and so has his grandfather. He is 17 and very angry. He does not feel loved and accepted. I have already tried long-distance QE with him when he is still asleep because he does not believe in these things. He was always very important to me, although I fear his temper, because when he gets angry, he screams loudly and hits the door. He is quite strong and looks already much older than he is. I am worried about him all the time. Do you think this is the thing for his case? I lost my hope somehow.

Answer: The first thing to remember is to make sure you are physically safe. QE will work wonders with angry and violent people but it usually takes time, especially if they are resistant to working with their problem. Safety first and then do QE.

Doing QE for your nephew has two very strong advantages; it will quell his anger over time and it will create a more peaceful, stable atmosphere within you. Not only is that good for you but it will also help him settle down when he is around you. It is like a subtle psychic protection that influences both of you in a very quiet level.

You should be doing Extended QE at least two times a day for 10–30 minutes each. Good times are before bed and upon waking, but anytime will work. You can also do shorter sessions as you feel the need.

23. Do you work with time travel or energy frequencies?

This year, I learned Matrix Energetics in Miami. Afterwards, I read your book. In fact, I've already read it twice. Thank you for a great and interesting book. Do you also work with time travel? Do you have some additional healing frequencies?

I ask you this because I found differences between QE and Matrix Energetics. Dr. Bartlett teaches these things but I know that time does not really exist. I appreciate the way you have presented the concept of stepping out of time. Thanks, in advance, for your answer and many greetings from Germany.

Answer: Time travel is really not a concern when we do the QE/pure awareness work. Once we experience pure awareness, we don't really need to do anything else. In fact, we can't do anything. Doing is an illusion, the result of a time-captured mind. So if you want to time travel, you must believe in the illusion of time. Practically, we all must work within the time illusion, but we don't have to believe it. Actually "believe" is not the right word. We can only step out of time when we are purely aware of pure awareness. Then life goes on as before but we are somehow beyond and within at the same no-time. In this case, the experience is worth a thousand words.

That said, once we are aware of pure awareness, there is no reason we can't play in the illusion. Life is fullness in pure awareness. Once you know pure awareness, then take time for energy work, or anything else for that matter. Pure awareness first, then everything else. Energy work by itself is great but baseless without direct perception of where energy comes from. Energy work without pure awareness tends to focus on energy and boundaries, forgetting the fullness of unboundedness.

24. Can I use an image instead of an intention?

Before practicing QE, I choose an intention. Why not simply imagine a positive picture of my client, full of joy and happiness? Doesn't choosing an intention mean I limit myself? Imagination includes so much more than precise words. You know, a picture is worth a thousand words.

Answer: Whether we use words or imagery for the intention, doesn't really matter. Eufeeling gets the picture even before it forms in our heads. When you form a clear picture of what you want, you actually limit solutions from outside that image. That is, you limit the number of possible solutions to the image you have formed. If that imagined resolution is not universally supportive, it will not manifest. You see, we get the idea that we are somehow helping Eufeeling find disharmony and then showing it how to fix that oversight on its part. This is a self-centered view that ignores the reality of universal harmony. In actuality, there is no disharmony. There is only the *idea* of good and evil, right and wrong, cooked up in our minds. There is no universal wrong. That also means that there can be no universal right. It is what it is. That is why we say in QE, "We take what we get." It keeps us from trying to control the outcome. Control is the main tool of ego and limits the outcome to a single intention.

When we are deep in stillness—free of restless desires to make lots of money or climb a bigger mountain—we are also free of the desire to heal. Isn't that so? Deep in peace the "valleys and the peaks" are leveled out. The impulse to heal is apparent but the desire to heal is gone. You lose the desire because you are already at peace. Neat, huh? The ultimate goal of every desire is to be aware of pure awareness. When you cut to the chase and go right to pure awareness, then desires dissolve into faint impulses of creativity in perfect harmony with universal wisdom. You can heal with very precise images or general ideas; it does not matter. You are not doing the healing and neither is the technique. All healing is apparent healing relative to our individual perspective at that time.

25. Can I do QE on food?
What about praying before eating?

Can I do QE to purify my food or make my vitamins more potent?

Answer: Of course, the same way you do it for anything else. Doing QE with food is great because it settles you down and prepares your digestion for the meal to come. It also helps to dispel the negativity around pesticides, hormones, and other toxins that work their way into your mind and food. If you pray before you eat, then do QE before you pray. You will be more settled and your prayer will be more effective.

26. Would QE have made my kitchen just how I wanted it?

After months of planning my new kitchen, it didn't turn out at all like I wanted it to. Would QE have made my kitchen just how I wanted it?

Answer: Nothing in life really turns out the way we want. When we do QE, *things* often turn out better and when they don't, we are more accepting because we are already enjoying the *ultimate reason we wanted a new kitchen*—peace in pure awareness. Ego takes a vacation.

In reality, we are not really in control of the outcome of our thoughts and actions. It just seems that way because ego does a pretty good job of convincing us otherwise. But when we think about it, not much in life ends up just like we plan. When we are aware of pure awareness, we purely observe as creation goes on about its business. We watch its wonders appear and have no need to take credit for ourselves.

27. How long should QE take to heal?

I've noticed that sometimes the QE healing comes in seconds and sometimes there is hardly a change even after five minutes. How long should QE take to heal?

Answer: QE isn't really healing. You are not really healing. Pure awareness isn't really healing. Healing appears to take place when your consciousness shifts from one reality—or, more accurately, illusion—to another. That's right, healing is a matter of conscious perception. The quality of our perceptions are determined by how much pure awareness we perceive. The more pure awareness we perceive, the more healing appears to take place. The shift from a limited consciousness to unbounded awareness opens us to an alternate realization that already existed but, until we opened to it, was unrealized. Wow, did I just let the cat out of the bag?

28. Why does QE work and then stop working?

I get great results with my clients and myself when I use QE. But sometimes those results only last a few days and then I have to do QE again. Why isn't the healing always permanent?

Answer: Healing is a matter of conscious perception. If pure awareness is clearly realized, then healing is permanent. If pure awareness is held for a few days, then healing is less permanent. Then the partner needs another shot of QE. That is, they need to be reminded about pure awareness.

Here is a very clear example of what I mean. A friend told me of a woman who asked him to do QE on her eyesight. She couldn't read the words on a printed page. He did QE for about two minutes and she was amazed when all the blurry squiggles swam into focus and she could read the page clearly. But before she finished reading to the end, all the letters became unfocused again. Her belief system did not fit her experience and she lost awareness of pure awareness and then clear sightedness. She will regain her clear eyesight with continued exposure to pure awareness. She already knows it is possible and that is a start. Now she only needs to spend more

time getting to know pure awareness. Her new friend (pure awareness) will dissolve her old belief systems automatically and without
effort, just like it did the first time.

29. Can QE increase my bank account?

*How can I use QE effectively to get more money on my bank account?
I do understand that QE does include abundance in other areas. I just
think that I might be able to speed up the process!*

Answer: The first question you should ask is, "Why do I
want more money?" Of course, if you are starving the answer is
obvious. But if you have enough, then why do you want more?
The ego, unaware of pure awareness, is driven by fear. Fear is the
root of all negative emotions and many of the positive ones. The
pursuit of happiness is many times the fleeing of fear. Your ego
can never get enough until it becomes united with pure awareness. Established firmly in pure awareness, your ego will expand
to infinity and fear of loss will drop away.

Now, what about cash in the coffer? Of course QE will help get
more money. The trick is to do QE for more money and then
totally forget about it. You can do it often but immediately after
the QE session (which may last 15 seconds to 15 minutes), go
about your life as usual. The forces of nature will begin to gather
around your intention and, in time, you will realize more money.
I can guarantee you of one thing: you will not get it how you
picture it or when you want it. In fact, wishing for it with a sense
of urgency will only slow down the process. Just do QE often and
forget about it. You will get much, much more than you expect.

30. Can I make reading books more efficient with QE?

Could we make reading books more efficient with QE? For instance, could we put one hand on the book, the other on the head, and then the intention: The content of this book is available to me at all times? I'm not joking!

Answer: I don't know of the "book to mind" technique. I would love to see it done. I am a slow reader and drawing specifics from a book in that way would be most powerful indeed. In QE, we don't look for specific information. We have a simple, *abstract* intention and then we let Eufeeling do the work. That way the organizing power of pure awareness is free to collect from all of creation to satisfy our needs. It knows more about what we need than we do. So satisfying specifics is actually a side effect of becoming aware of pure awareness. QE will quell the ego and it is the ego that most of the time wants specifics like power and knowledge—the two forces of the universe. There is nothing wrong with the pursuit of specific knowledge unless it is done without being aware of pure awareness. That is when you know that you don't know. In QE we say, "Knowledge is ignorance."

It is wonderful that you think in this way and I'm glad you are not kidding. We are all confined, fenced in by our beliefs and unsupported perceptions; unsupported by pure awareness. I haven't been able to QE a book and absorb the content effortlessly but maybe you can. QE opens our awareness to unlimited possibilities. The only restrictions are those we place on ourselves. That doesn't mean that we can throw off the yoke of ignorance whenever we like. We just don't want to fight against what is. We want to allow the wisdom of awareness to gift us this incredible world as it is. That is greater than any knowledge contained in any book.

Even the great saints remained chained to the confines of convention. For the most part, they still felt frustration, sadness, and concern; got colds and joint aches; and, except for the most current, have died. The difference between them and the rest of humanity is that they were anchored in pure awareness; they did not suffer. So whether they could soak up knowledge with a damp sponge or not, they were at peace with whatever came their way.

So go for it. QE a book for its knowledge or spread your wings and fly to the moon. You may surprise all of us stuck in our everyday minds. You would not be the first to do so. But one thing is for certain. When you do QE, your chances of breaking the bonds that chain you to mediocrity are much greater than not. And even if you don't achieve what you set out to do, you will still have pure awareness, more valuable than anything you could possibly own or do.

31. Can I know everything by being in pure awareness?

I understand your writing about the ego wanting to control and gain power, but, on the other hand, I think that spirituality should be somehow applicable in our daily life. So the question is, if I am preparing for an exam, what is the difference if I learn in the traditional way, the hard way, or if I let the pure awareness do the work? My understanding of the consciousness is that it knows everything so it is just a matter of tuning in to the information.

Answer: You are right to say that everything is available to us on some level of creation. It is just a matter of finding the right way to look and find that information. There are many techniques to do this; contact the Akashic Records and other subtle bodies of knowledge. However, this is not QE. QE simply allows us to be aware of pure awareness so that whatever we do, we do better, and with more joy, compassion, and love. If you want to absorb information from a book, perform QE first and then do a technique for knowledge. This is how spirituality is "applicable in daily life."

I'm not sure how you are defining consciousness. For me, consciousness is a focused awareness not to be confused with pure awareness. Pure awareness is apparent consciousness but consciousness is not pure awareness. Pure awareness transcends all and includes all without being touched. Anyway, before we get too wrapped up in defining the indefinable, let's just say that you can't use pure awareness like energy. It is beyond energy and form. Practically speaking, just become aware of pure awareness and then do what you feel needs to be done. In reality, you are not doing anything anyway. It just appears that way. But that is another story for another time.

32. How can I overcome my ego with QE?

I've been learning and practicing energy work for about five years. I've learned EFT, TAT, Body Talk, Quantum Touch, Healing Codes, Jin Shin Jyutsu, Yuen Method, and a little Matrix Energetics (which seems very similar to QE). I normally practice on 2–5 friends or family members daily. I think I need more help with working on getting rid of my ego, being detached from the results, not taking things person-ally when the results are not as good as I would like them to be, devel-oping more intuition; not seeing/feeling separate from anyone, and increasing love and compassion for people. I've worked with some Matrix Energetics practitioners and Yuen practitioners who are very intuitive and would like to be able to do what they do, or be able to do what you do. I'd like to increase the Eufeeling and be more aware of the Awareness, not only because of the energy work I do, but also for my spiritual growth, which, when all is said and done, is the real reason we're all here.

Answer: You have told me that you are involved with many different healing techniques. It might be a good idea to ask yourself why you have studied so many systems in such a short time. What is the impulse behind the drive? It appears that all this activity has left you a little frustrated as seen by your desire to become more spiritual. Oddly enough, healing comes from stillness, not activity. No technique, QE included, ever healed. For that matter, no person has ever healed. Healing only comes from Eufeeling and Eufeeling is not an activity but a state of being; an awareness of absolute stillness. All great healers draw from the stillness within. It might be time for you, with all your knowledge of healing techniques, to now turn your consciousness toward pure awareness and see what happens without conscious control. All the things you would like to have—getting rid of ego, being unattached to results, increasing love and compassion—are obtained by non-attachment, by letting go. The QE process is successful when it stops working; when the practitioner stands still in pure awareness and becomes witness to what then unfolds. From the vantage point of silent observation, one cannot be attached to results and can only feel compassion, love, and bliss—the Eufeeling. It does not matter what technique is employed. Success or failure will be determined by the degree of pure awareness that is reflected in the healer's awareness.

Your experience with QE left you feeling "peaceful and relaxed," enjoying a "subtle energy." This is the foundation for healing. In fact, it is the foundation for any activity be it spiritual, physical, mental, social, etc. Maintain pure awareness more and more and your life will fall more and more in accord with your natural tendencies.

33. Will QE help me in my next life?

For three years I walked only with crutches and only ten steps very, very slowly. Doctors say that I have multiple scleroses. In my soul there is power and lightness always. And I am positive all the time in spite of my pain. My mother said to me that I will not be healthy in this life but maybe in my next life. I hope she is not right. I would be so happy if I can be healthy, walking without crutches and playing the piano again. Please, can you help me?

Answer: I do not put much stock in past/next lives. The one right in front of me is plenty enough for me. Keep doing QE on yourself but, more importantly, do it for others. Give this wonderful gift to others and your inner healing will evolve remarkably. Make sure you re-read this book while you are doing QE for others. Then—and this is very important—stop trying to heal. You will only push it away. Focus on the joys you *do* have and do QE. What healing you experience will be effortless. How much healing takes place we will just have to wait and see, but removing your psychological suffering will free you for maximum physical healing.

34. Can I mix QE with other techniques?

I started to learn Transcendental Meditation (TM) about two weeks ago. In your book I've seen that you also practiced TM for a long time. Is it possible to use TM in combination with your healing technique?

Answer: It is true, I did TM for some years and I am very grateful to Maharishi for his teachings, especially the deep wisdom of Science of Creative Intelligence from which I draw much worth. But QE and TM should not be mixed together. Do not combine QE with any other technique. Do QE first and then any technique you do after that will work better. TM is a good sit-down technique. Use QE like an active meditation. Do it all day long and don't look for results. Just do it and go on and QE the next activity. Quickly you will find that evenness and easiness will grow, and aggravation and disharmony will begin to fade away. It's pretty amazing that you don't have to try for these things. Just doing QE brings them about completely without effort. In fact, they will not happen any other way. So, QE before TM, and QE before eating, bathing, and sleeping. QE, QE, QE! How simple can that be? (Hey, that's poetry!)

35. Can I remove ego by giving thanks to others?

I like to give thanks and gratitude to Source, Archangel Raphael, or whomever. It keeps my ego out of the way. What is your modus operandi?

Answer: You can't really remove ego by using the mind, the ego's playground. The very idea of removing the ego could be an egotistic desire spawned by a clever ego pulling the strings in the background. Even good deeds can have egoistic origins. The only safe way to eliminate egocentric thought and action is to go beyond the mind and let pure awareness do the thinking and acting. That is why we do not look for results. We simply bring our awareness to pure awareness, step back, and let life unfold before us. The "us" in this case is the "I" founded in pure awareness and not the ego manipulating the mind

36. Can QE cure cancer?

I have cancer and I also have a great deal of difficulty breathing. I am very worried about my condition and I wonder if QE can cure my cancer.

Answer: First of all, QE doesn't cure anything. Doctors don't cure and medicines don't cure. It is Eufeeling born of awareness of pure awareness that cures. Your problems have two parts to them: a) the situation like cancer or breathing, and b) how you feel about that situation. If we feel negatively about a situation, that is what makes it a problem. It is the emotional attachment to a condition that I consider a problem and that creates suffering. QE brings awareness of pure awareness and pure awareness works on both levels—the physical condition and the emotional attachment. Usually something like breathing responds very quickly to QE and cancer more slowly but that is not always the case. Your best course of action for both your worries and your cancer is to do QE for others as much as you can and have others do QE for you. Look toward living and let pure awareness take care of the rest.

Of course, always consult with your primary healthcare professional for guidance and treatment of your condition.

37. Why can't I keep pure awareness?

I have been working hard to apply QE in my daily life for all my problems. I do QE and get pure awareness but I can't keep it. What am I doing wrong?

Answer: Pure awareness does not have to be found because it is already there. You only need to become aware of it. As soon as you become aware of it by doing QE, your mind says, "Now I must keep it." That is the formula for failure. That is when you stop doing QE and let your mind take over again. You are trying too hard to "see" it or experience it. Stop trying; stop using your mind to figure out what is happening. Your mind just gets in the way.

Go back and do the "stop your thinking" exercise where you ask yourself the question, "Where will my next thought come from?" You will notice a pause in your thinking, a kind of momentary stop in thinking. In that gap, there is nothing, but you are still aware, right? No thoughts or feelings—just a stoppage of thought. In that nothing, you are still aware, right? You are aware without thought. That is pure awareness. But you don't even have to keep your thoughts away because you can have pure awareness and thoughts, too, as well as emotions and even activity. Anything you can have without being aware of pure awareness you can have with pure awareness. Don't try and figure it out. Your mind will never understand it. That is why QE is so incredible. It takes your awareness to pure awareness without your having to figure it out. You just do QE and you are there. You just do QE and.........

APPENDIX B
The Story of Nothing and How It Is Changing the World

As a boy, I lived in post-World War II Japan. I remember doing the things that all boys love: catching bees in a jar, making forts with rocks and sticks in the dirt and laying on my back watching puffy white clouds slide across a deep cerulean sky. The child's eye is the saint's eye. But that all changes, doesn't it? It was at this time that I had my first spiritual awakening. I had become discouraged and angry with my practice of judo. Sitting, frustrated and fuming on the tatami mat, my sensei taught me a mind-over-matter technique that drained me of anger and filled me with inner quiet. I was surprised by joy.

All through my adolescence and young adulthood, I read about and practiced yoga and breathing and meditation. I was able to keep alive the child's eye even as I went to college, married, and started a family. In the early 1970s, I became a teacher of Transcendental Meditation and studied the Science of Creative Intelligence (SCI) under the gentle guidance of Maharishi Mahesh Yogi. Later, SCI became the foundation for deeper exploration into the realm beyond the mind—pure awareness.

For 15 years, I deeply dedicated myself to spiritual exploration. My daily routine included 3½ hours of meditation, with additional time devoted to studying and teaching spiritual practices. I accumulated more than 2½ years of silent, deep meditation literally sequestered on mountain tops in the French and Swiss Alps for months at a time. The driving force behind my dedication was that most exalted and utterly elusive state of enlightenment. I felt that I could become enlightened by strength of will and austere and obscure practices.

During this time, I had many deep and meaningful spiritual experiences. I began to resonate on finer and finer levels of existence. I spent time learning on the level of angels. I sat in on the teachings of the ascended masters. I found the form of God and watched it dissolve into the formless essence of God-stuff. Ultimately, I became aware of pure awareness, the all-permeating Nothing from which all is born and into which all dissolves again.

I found myself with a foot in two worlds—the competitive world of day-to-day living and the etherial realms of subtle beings and soft surrender. It was not an easy time for me physically or emotionally. It was difficult to remain focused on my family and profession when the serene silence of the "other" world lay beckoning from every shimmering form.

In the late 1980s, I met with a small group of spiritual seekers to study and practice meditative techniques. It was at that time that I started receiving instruction from my disincarnate teacher, the destroyer of ignorance, Siva. I passed the techniques along to the group and we practiced them and passed them along to others. These techniques were the precursors to Quantum Entrainment (QE). We could heal, give readings, and even encourage the experience of peace in others. I taught for seven years but when I looked inwardly to see if I had moved any closer to enlightenment, I could not honestly say that I had. I looked at those following my teachings and found that they could inspire healing and interest in esoteric practices but they, too, failed to show me any significant inner growth. So, in the mid-1990s, I walked away from my students and my teachings and began to look deeply inside for an answer to my life long quest for freedom from suffering.

I decided to remove anything from my life that did not encourage enlightenment. I began removing everything that did not work. It was a process that lasted seven more years. This time became the most painful of my life. During that time, I ended a 30-year marriage, gave up my teaching, dissolved my chiropractic practice, fell in and out of love, and moved away from friends and family to a city where I was virtually alone. It was then that I began writing *Beyond Happiness: How You Can Fulfill Your Deepest Desire*.

I discovered during that time that nothing I had done was working. In my new home, alone and without direction, I became very ill. I laid in bed day after day under the dark cloud of depression while my body finally succumbed to the accumulated years of stress and disappointment. I developed physical maladies that drained me and made it impossible to think clearly. I could not write for ten months.

During the time of deepest darkness, I had a remarkable awakening unlike any I had experienced before. It stood out like a beacon in the blackness of night. In a single flash of insight, I cognized that nothing moves; that all created things and thoughts are non-moving reflections of pure awareness. In fact, in some way I cannot explain, form does not exist. Form and movement are one and the same non-moving emptiness. Any effort to explain this experience is laughably inadequate. Whether I can explain this cognition or not, it resonates deep within the stillness that is my essence (not my essence but the Essence). It is from here that I think and work and love and cry. It was at this time that the mechanics of creation began to open to my awareness. It is from here that QE was born and I began to learn to heal.

It took some years more before the full impact of my cognition took hold. In fact, I am still watching the process unfold. It is as if the reflection of pure awareness I call "me" has to be infused with fullness slowly over apparent time. And so, without effort I have observed a quiet metamorphosis from the inside out. All the while I am both at peace and in apparent turmoil. My life is as it was before. I get frustrated, angry, sad, and happy. I become temporarily overshadowed by the human condition but return quickly and without effort renewed to inner quiet like a pristine meadow after a summer thundershower. But my life—or, more accurately, this life—is also unfathomable, free from form and function; free to be...nothing.

I kept saying to myself that nothing works. Then I realized that nothing did work. That is the "nothing" of pure awareness is the only thing that works and that is because it is nothing. All the time I was meditating and reading and teaching, I had a goal to be free of suffering. As long as I had a goal, then I wasn't satisfied where I was. You see? A goal creates a path and a path takes you away from where you are. But my cognition showed that the nothing of pure awareness is everywhere, all the time. That is, there is nowhere to go and nothing you can do to get peace because it is already where you are. You can't get something you already have. All you need to do is become aware that you have it, right? A goal and a path are illusions. They take the mind away from non-moving awareness and involve it in the illusory world of good and bad, right and wrong, fleeting happiness and ultimate suffering.

So herein lies the core of my teaching: You do not need to do anything to be aware of pure awareness. You already have pure awareness so you only need to become aware of it. All the time I spent in deep meditation and studying to become free of suffering only deepened my suffering. It was not needed. Only awareness of pure awareness is needed to be free and that is the simplest thing in existence.

Not quite two years ago, I was quietly contemplating the plight of humanity on Earth. I wondered how our suffering might be replaced with the inner peace that has been extolled throughout the ages by saints and sages alike. I wondered why so many of us turn outward—away from inner bliss—to embrace the fleeting pleasures of the senses. It was that simple inquiry that opened my consciousness to the genius of what I would later call QE. Please know that I take no credit for this insight. I don't even take authorship for asking the question. In reality, both the question and the answer are superfluous but that is a story for another time.

What I realized was that our wayward minds have to somehow be excited about something before they will pay proper attention. So I offered the mind the thought of instant healing. That got it interested initially but the problem is that the nothing of pure awareness is not exciting to our minds. Actually, our senses can never experience pure awareness and our minds will never understand it. So, what can we do? My challenge was to interest the mind in something that could not be experienced and teach it something that could not be understood. Then the mind had to remain in this non-experience state of pure awareness long enough to feel the harmonious effects on body and mind. This would have to be a very fast process for the mind is extremely restless. The answer was given in the form of the Eufeeling, a stroke of utter genius. The Eufeeling balances the mind between the absolute non-movement of pure awareness and its impulsive, constant activity. The Eufeeling holds the mind there until not only the initiator's body/mind benefits but also the partner she is working with. It was a most remarkable and completely unique idea. I couldn't wait to try it out.

I did try it out and was overwhelmed at the speed and the depth of healing of this new process. Next I tried to teach it and found that others could learn the QE process as quickly and easily as the process was practiced. Several months after discovering QE, I wrote *The Secret of Instant Healing* so that people around the world could learn how to experience pure awareness through healing.

As I write this, the German translation of *The Secret of Instant Healing*, (*Quantenheilung*) has been the number one selling book in both the Natural Healing and Esoteric categories for the last seven months with no indication of letting up. This was achieved by word of mouth, and the word continues to spread. The rest of Europe—indeed, the rest of the world from Australia to Austria, Angola to Estonia—is beginning to awaken to the joyful potential of QE. *The Secret of Instant Healing* will also be published in Spanish and Czech and a number of other countries soon.

All in all, the growth of QE has been phenomenal when you consider it was born just two years ago and is still in its infancy. Then again, it shouldn't be surprising because one of the first intentions I cradled in my mind after developing QE was for the rapid spread of QE and, with it, harmony in this world. It seems that the future of QE is tied to the future fortune of our world. The particulars of world peace, ecological instability, poverty, and the like have no simple solution, at least not by working on the same level of disharmony that created them. Discordant thinking must necessarily reflect discordant action. The answer to world harmony is not in the particulars but in the realization of our very inner, harmonious nature. Just as the insidious nature of chaotic thinking has weakened our world, so, too, the nurturing rays of Self can heal it. I believe that QE will add the necessary spiritual leverage to create the tipping point for peace. Then we will achieve, as a whole, what only a few isolated luminaries have so far realized. We will be at rest, complete, reflecting perfect harmony in a world at peace with its Self.

Glossary

Bliss—See Eufeeling

Consciousness (Conscious awareness, Common awareness)—Perception of the relative world without Self-awareness. The apparent flow of pure awareness through the narrow confines of the mind. When consciousness awareness turns inward and becomes aware of Self, it becomes Self-aware.

Desire—A desire is ego-driven emotion. It is something you feel you want or need to make some part of you more complete. Desires spring out of memory and bring with them a host of supporting thoughts and emotions. They create action designed to fulfill the desire. That action only creates more and stronger desires.

Ego—Ego arises when mind forgets it is Self. It is the controlling entity of the unaware mind. It is born of fear which is both its foil and its fuel. It wants to be whole and merge with Self but fears assimilation by Self. Ego tries to eliminate what it cannot control. It feels that if it can control everything, it can be whole. It is the primal cause of suffering. Time, fear, and ego are one and the same. Ego is an illusion. Self-awareness eliminates ego's destructive influence over the mind not by destroying it but expanding it to infinity.

Eufeeling—Eufeelings are feelings that are pure and unconditional. They are the natural state of a mind that is aware of its Self. At first, they appear to be hierarchical, but each is a different flavor of Self in the mind. The apparent hierarchy begins with stillness and then evolves to peace, joy, bliss, ecstasy, and then complete immersion in the indescribable. Eufeelings can produce feelings. Feelings cannot produce Eufeelings. (Synonymous with Self)

Fear—Fear is the spark that is created when mind separates from Self. Fear is the sum total of all your feelings, including happiness and pleasure. It is the primal motivator of the Self-separated mind. (Synonymous with time and ego)

Feelings—Feelings are conditional. All feelings come from the primal feeling fear. Fear creates insecurity, which produces the corresponding feeling, thought, and action. Feelings are associated with psychological time. When fear manifests in the past, it produces feelings of guilt, revenge, self-pity, remorse, sadness, etc. Perceived as the future, fear produces feelings of tension, dread, worry, pride, etc. Anger is the first expression of fear and is also expressed in both the future and the past. Happiness, excitement, delight, and even love are fear-based conditional feelings. Feelings can produce other feelings. They cannot produce Eufeeling.

God—the definition of God changes with the level of consciousness awareness. In conscious awareness, God has energy and form. When Self-aware, God is the creator. When aware of pure awareness, God is not.

"I"—See Self

I Am—See Self

Intuition—The expression of Self in the phenomenal world. Self-awareness. (Synonymous with Wisdom)

Knowing—When Self becomes aware of itself, that is Knowing. The transition from knowing to Knowing is Self-awareness. Knowing tenderly nurtures, guides, and protects us. This is what we call intuition. Intuition is the tender expression of the Self reflected in the mind. Intuition is Knowing without analysis and logic while it enriches and supports both. Intuition is Knowing that Nothing has everything under control.

Knowledge—Knowledge is the result of gathering data which adds to our understanding. Knowledge is a synthesis of understanding and experience. It is relative and changes with time and circumstances. Knowledge is ignorance.

Love – See Eufeeling

"Me"—Everything that makes a person unique is "me." "Me" is made of thoughts and emotions, experiences, memories, hopes, and fears. "Me" changes over your lifetime.

Momentum—The state where Self-awareness is automatically reestablished when it is lost.

Nothing—Nothing cannot be understood. Nothing is not empty. Nothing is not separate from what is created from It. It is Its creation. Everything is Nothing. Nothing only appears as the phenomenal world. Pure awareness is Nothing. When one becomes aware of pure awareness, one knows Nothing which is to Not-Know. One must know Nothing to know Self.

Not-Knowing—Not-Knowing is awareness of Nothing. When Self drops away, leaving only pure awareness, that is Not-Knowing. The advantage of the Not-Knower is that of knowing no movement and no other. No movement means It is timeless and no other means It is One. Not-Knowing has nowhere to go and nothing to do. The illusion of going and doing has been exposed. It is free to be. Not-Knowing is the realization of absolute unity. (See Pure Awareness.)

Observe—See Witness

Peace – See Eufeeling

Pure Awareness—The highest Knowing. Awareness of that which is unchanging, without beginning or end. Awareness of Nothing. When aware of pure awareness, one realizes that creation is an illusion. (See Not-Knowing.) One Knows without understanding that everything, past, present, and future exists simultaneously. One realizes that there is no movement. Every created thing is the unmoving, non-existent illusion of pure awareness.

Pure Being—Pure being is pure awareness. Since pure awareness is everywhere at once, it does not move and is therefore pure being.

Pure Consciousness—Awareness of no-thinking, the gap between thoughts.

Pure Love—Pure love is pure awareness reflected through the clear lens of Self. Awareness that falls equally on all things, sees no opposites, has no point of view and creates no disharmony.

Psychological Time—Psychological time is the cause of all problems facing human kind. The mind that is not aware of the present vacillates between the past and future, neither of which exists. This vacillation creates the illusion of movement we call time. Problems arise when we mistake the illusion for the truth. The mind firmly set on the present is at rest, breaking the illusion of movement and removing the cause of suffering.

Self—Self is unbounded and beyond time. It is aware without movement. Self manifests on the silent ocean of pure awareness when there is something to observe. When it becomes aware of its own existence, it becomes aware of pure love. The symptom of consciousness becoming aware of Self is inner peace. It is the unchanging part of you that was there in childhood, adolescence, and adulthood, watching but never interfering, untouched but supporting all that you are. In the beginning, it is the silent witness of your life. In the end, the wave of Self realizes that there is nothing to observe but Self and settles back into the ocean of pure awareness.

Self-Awareness—Awareness of that unbounded, eternal aspect of life from which the mind/body/environment is created. In its simplest state, it is recognized as the gap between thoughts. Complete realization of Self comes upon its dissolution into pure awareness. At this point, no separate Self can be observed as all things are equal in their expression of pure awareness. Self is synonymous with God, the formless creator.

Spiritual—The perception and practice of becoming aware of Self.

Surrender—Surrender means we relinquish hope and are not looking to the future for things to get better. It is not "giving up." It means opening our awareness to Self and waiting to see what options will issue forth from that state of infinite possibilities. Surrender recognizes Self as the answer to all problems.

Wisdom—The expression of Self in the phenomenal world; Intuition.

Witness—The witness is a door through which common consciousness must go to find pure awareness. The witness is the Self. In light, witnessing the witness is distinctly separate from objects and activity. In the fuller stages of witnessing, the witness begins to recognize the stillness of Self in objects and activity. Finally, the witness loses its individuality and merges into pure awareness. (Synonymous with Observer)

Frank welcomes your comments and questions.
He can be contacted at:
Website:www.QuantumEntrainment.com
E-mail: info@QuantumEntrainment.com

Breinigsville, PA USA
12 August 2010
243512BV00001B/76/P